COMMUNITY CAPITALISM

by RICHARD P. TAUB

Harvard Business School Press

Boston, Massachusetts

Originally published in hardcover by the Harvard
Business School Press, 1988

© 1988, 1994 by the President and Fellows of Harvard College
All rights reserved.
Printed in the United States of America

98 97 96 95 94   5 4 3 2 1

Library of Congress Cataloging-in-Publication Data

Taub, Richard P.
   Community capitalism / by Richard P. Taub.
      p.   cm.
   Bibliography: p. 145.
   Includes index.
   ISBN 0-87584-553-3 (pbk.: alk. paper)
   1. Shorebank Corporation (Chicago, Ill.)   2. Community
development. Urban—Illinois—Chicago—Case studies.   3. Community
development corporations—Illinois—Chicago—Case studies.   4. South
Shore (Chicago, Ill.)   I. Title.
HN90.C6T38   1988
307.7'6'06077311—dc19   87-35373
                                                                    CIP

Contents

Preface to the Paperback Edition

In October 1993, the directors of the Shorebank Corporation combined their semiannual meeting with the company's twentieth birthday party. In honor of the occasion, they held the event at Couchwood, a lakeside family estate located between Malvern and Hot Springs, Arkansas.

This site was chosen for its proximity to the bank's first development effort outside the state of Illinois. From 1973 to 1988, Shorebank had concentrated on rebuilding the South Shore community in Chicago; success there led to increased public attention and, ultimately, an invitation from then Arkansas governor Bill Clinton and the Winthrop Rockefeller Foundation to launch a similar program in the southern part of that state. Couchwood is 35 miles northeast of Arkadelphia, the home of the Southern Development Bancorporation (known as Southern), whose operation closely replicates the structure of its parent in Chicago.

The dramatic contrasts between the south side of Chicago and southwestern Arkansas help illustrate the range and reach of Shorebank enterprises today and the new development problems they confront. The meeting at Couchwood provides a vantage point from which to assess the impact of Shorebank's achievements and consider the prospects for extending its development model to other communities.

When I first wrote *Community Capitalism*, I was tempted to call the South Shore Bank "The Little Bank That Could," recalling the children's story of the little locomotive that faced the challenge of pulling a long circus train up a steep hill. Functioning in relative obscurity and committed to a goal—community revitalization—that many knowledgeable people thought was quixotic, the South Shore Bank initially had difficulty raising capital and deposits. Although its resources seemed incommensurate with the task at hand, through extraordinary effort and inventiveness its management did indeed succeed.

By 1993, the South Shore Bank and its management team probably received as much positive public attention as any bank in the the country. Perhaps because the creation of similar organizations became a key element of Bill Clinton's presidential campaign, capital—not always easy to raise—began to flow in after his election, and other cities and regions around the country and throughout the world asked Shorebank's management to come to their aid.

NEW INITIATIVES

By the time of the twentieth anniversary meeting, the outlines of the Shorebank enterprise had taken a distinctively new shape. The company was operating four programs outside Chicago, was considering several new projects, and had extended its activities in Chicago. In describing these programs it is important to note that community development takes time. Although the Shorebank organization in Chicago had many individual successes to its credit, its managers had to learn what worked and then to mobilize resources appropriately. It was eight years before there was clear evidence that the South Shore had been turned around. Because the company was able to maintain an adequate capital base, it was free to experiment, learn, and grow. As Shorebank extends its activities into radically different communities, its staff will inevitably make adjustments as they learn to understand the dynamics of new environments. They need time to build fresh networks of personal ties in order to establish trust and the proper levels of communication. As these new initiatives unfold, we will learn more about Shorebank's abilities to serve as a model for community development and revitalization.

South Arkansas

As noted, the Southern Development Bancorporation operates in a region that could hardly be more different from Chicago's south side. South Shore covers roughly a square mile of land and has a population of about 75,000; Southern's territory is 32 counties, with 600,000 residents spread over 20,000 square miles. While South Shore's population is almost entirely African-American, the proportion of the minority population in South Arkansas varies from 60 to 20 percent as one moves from east to west. The physical reality of South Shore is mainly pavement and buildings, while South Arkansas is mainly forest, occasionally broken up by farms, rivers, lakes, and small towns. When Shorebank extended its Chicago activities to the neighborhood of Austin, some staffers complained about the ten-mile commute. Southern staffers may travel 200 miles from Arkadelphia to pursue their development activities.

These demographic differences contribute to different development priorities and challenges in the two regions. Because South Shore is located within a prosperous metropolitan region, a large part of the revitalization effort has involved channeling nearby resources back into a community that had been short-changed as its composition changed from white to black. The emphasis has been on providing credit and investing in deteriorating multiple-family dwellings to encourage South Shore residents to think about their property in a more entrepreneurial way. By contrast, South Arkansas—along with its neighbors, Louisiana and Mississippi—is one of the poorest regions of the country. Its low population density means that residents are far from markets for their products and from capital markets—that is, sources of investment. Southern staffers are not only concerned with community development but with improving an entire regional economy.

Nevertheless, Shorebank's structural model has successfully been implemented in South Arkansas. In addition to running the full-service Elk Horn Bank, Southern operates four subsidiaries:

- *Opportunity Lands*. This for-profit real estate company has converted vacant storefronts in downtown Arkadelphia into office centers, contributing dramatically to the revitalization of a dying business district. The company has also rehabilitated blocks of rental housing on the edges of Pine Bluff's and Helena's business districts, and additional projects for both towns are in the pipeline.

- *Southern Ventures*. This for-profit venture capital company made equity investments available to promising start-ups or successful small companies attempting to grow quickly. A high-risk enterprise, whose management expected the many losses of high-risk deals to be more than offset by a few big winners, Southern Ventures appeared at the time of this writing to be winding down after suffering larger losses than expected. This failure may have resulted from inadequate capitalization and an unwillingness to combine shorter-term, income-producing debt instruments with long-term equity investments.

- *Arkansas Enterprise Group.* This was conceived as a source of technical assistance and seed capital (small and relatively more risky loans than a bank would provide for start-ups). So far, AEG has made loans to existing companies that had difficulty getting credit from conventional sources. It has not yet discovered a method to provide technical assistance to large numbers of entrepreneurs in a cost-effective way, in part because many local entrepreneurs, normally a stubborn lot, may also resist taking advice from outsiders.

- *Good Faith Fund.* This is the only Southern company that does not have a Chicago counterpart. Based on a model from Bangladesh to help the very poor escape from their poverty through self-employment, the fund focuses on peer-group lending for microenterprises, the smallest kind of businesses. The most innovative of Southern's programs, the Good Faith Fund had difficulty importing the model to South Arkansas, where loans do not carry the same life-or-death urgency as they do in Bangladesh. Consequently, initial loan volume was low and delinquencies were high. However, through tenacity and constant innovation, the program is beginning to reverse these early setbacks.

In its first five years, Southern has lent or invested about $45 million (of which $23 million is explicitly classified as development lending) to 679 small business customers. Learning how to accomplish development in a rural and southern setting has taken some time, but the company already has an impressive record.

Michigan

Although the Shorebank mission statement asserts that Shorebank is primarily an urban development company, much of its expansion efforts have been into rural areas. Not long after establishing the Southern Development Bancorporation, Shorebank teamed up with an innovative technical assistance provider at Northern Michigan University in Marquette, to create a partnership between the Northern Economic Initiatives Company and the North Coast Bidco (business and industrial development company)—the former to provide technical assistance and the latter to provide loans. In response to the decline of its major industry, automobile manufacturing, Michigan conceived this program to boost development by arranging for loans to developers to turn into equity capital if the developer creates jobs. This is the first Shorebank program where the government provided a substantial part of the company's capital. In late 1993, after a year and a half of operation, NEIC-North Coast Bidco appeared to have achievements that are, by and large, a mirror image of Southern's—the technical assistance component is busy working with furniture manufacturing companies on design innovation and plans to visit industry trade shows, while the lending arm of the organization has made few loans.

Kansas City
   The third enterprise outside of Chicago is not yet, strictly speaking, a development effort. Shorebank's management was invited to help turn around a failing minority-run bank in Kansas City. The bank's economic situation is improving.

Poland
   Shorebank's fourth major out-of-town enterprise is a program designed to make small business loans and teach Polish bankers how to make and administer loans themselves. Under contract to the Polish-American Enterprise Fund, Shorebank's "Windows" program, named for the loan windows it opened in Polish banks, has approved 2,400 loans for more than $58 million. Having achieved the goal of training Polish lenders and supervisors, the program is now mostly in Polish hands.

New Projects
   In addition to these four programs, two projects—one rural and one urban—were about to get under way in late 1993. The rural project is unique for Shorebank in that its primary focus is environmental protection—providing economic opportunities for local residents by encouraging them to produce products from renewable

resources and helping local business people market these products. Shorebank's partner will be Ecotrust, a Portland, Oregon-based, not-for-profit organization whose main interest is to preserve the Pacific Northwest ecosystem.

Shorebank and Ecotrust chose the Willapa Bay Area in southwestern Washington as the program's site. This region contains a series of small, economically marginal towns whose income is derived from the sea and nearby extensive forests. The first stage in the process will be to establish an affiliate whose initial charge will be similar to that of the Arkansas Enterprise Group—stimulating business growth through technical and marketing assistance and provision of credit. Ultimately, Shorebank plans to create a bank holding company, First Environmental Bancorporation, which would provide development banking services from northern California to Alaska. As the South Shore Bank in Chicago attracted "development deposits" from a national constituency of people concerned about urban problems, Shorebank hopes to appeal to individuals and foundations concerned about environmental issues by creating "eco-deposits."

In early 1994, Shorebank plans to establish a subsidiary in Cleveland. This operation will include a bank and other development-oriented units. So far, a real estate development corporation modeled on City Lands in Chicago and a business development company similar to AEG in Arkansas, but relying more heavily on business incubators, are planned. Cleveland Tomorrow, a private sector leadership group, will help raise two-thirds of the $17.5 million necessary for the enterprise.

Milwaukee and Detroit are also candidates for future Shorebank programs. In these cities, as in Cleveland, local business leaders with political support play a role in recruiting the Shorebank Company and offering to raise capital and provide other assistance. The Milwaukee enterprise has undergone more extensive evaluation than has Detroit's. Other cities continue to approach Shorebank management, the most recent being Baltimore. It is too early to tell how those activities will play out.

There is continuing international interest in Shorebank as well. In 1993, Shorebank began discussions with the Bulgarian government about setting up a development bank in Bulgaria, and the European Bank for Reconstruction and Development began to explore the possibility of establishing a program in Russia similar to the one in Poland. Three Shorebank officials have already visited some provincial Russian towns to assess the possibilities for such a program.

Chicago

While noting Shorebank activities since the initial publication of this book, we should not overlook the increased range of its Chicago programs. In 1988, the organization opened a branch of the South Shore Bank in Austin, a low-income minority neighborhood of about five square miles, with a population of approximately 110,000. By the time the South Shore Bank entered Austin, the community was more seriously deteriorated than South Shore ever was. The Austin branch is not a full-service bank—it makes loans but takes only CDs as deposits; it provides mortgages for the purchase and rehabilitation of the small housing units that mainly characterize the neighborhood. The bank has also created a mortgage product to compete with traditional mortgage companies, that create a vicious cycle by offering mortgages to underqualified buyers and foreclosing on these mortgages, thereby contributing to high property turnover and increased deterioration. By mid-1993, the Austin branch had committed approximately $45 million to housing-related loans, becoming the single largest lender in the neighborhood, with about 20 percent of the mortgage market.

At the time the Austin branch opened, two Shorebank subsidiaries—City Lands and The Neighborhood Institute—also entered the neighborhood aggressively. They purchased large, deteriorated apartment buildings from a tax reactivation sale, corralling Section 8 subsidies and committing themselves to the restoration of some of the most deteriorated multifamily dwellings in the neighborhood. These two subsidiaries have participated in the rehabilitation of 644 units in some 25 buildings.

Another Shorebank team has developed the Austin Labor Force Intermediary, a complex program that proposes to bring together an array of existing community agencies and service providers to help prepare individuals enter the labor market and support local businesses that might employ them. This project got under way in late 1993.

Is Austin a definably better community for all the work and capital outlay that have been committed to it over the past five years? On that question, the jury is still out. A detailed research program, tentatively scheduled for completion in 1994, may provide a sharper picture of Shorebank's achievements. What is indisputable is that the high levels of initial deterioration, the overall decline in opportunities for low-income minority workers, and the problems created by drugs and crime make this effort particularly difficult.

Shorebank now has an ambitious plan to develop much of Chicago's South Side outside of South Shore. The plan reflects a growing concern among Shorebank's managers that the company's projected expansion into other regions will divert attention from the original site of its development programs. The new effort will be financed in part by $10 million in new capital, most of which was provided by a group of Chicago's largest banks in 1993.

THE ROLE OF GOVERNMENT

All of these programs have been pursued without the direct intervention of the federal government. Although government resources have played a role in Shorebank's endeavors—the Bidco in Michigan, Small Business Administration and federal and state housing agency subsidies everywhere, for example—the financing and motivation have come almost exclusively from foundations, other private sector groups, and individuals. This may be about to change. It is possible, for example, that some communities will solicit Shorebank's services on the assumption that President Clinton's public support of the organization's efforts will translate into federal financial support.

This perception is not unrealistic. Since the presidential campaign—when Clinton singled out the South Shore Bank as a model for achieving economic development—the connections between the administration and the bank have strengthened. Shorebank and Southern representatives attended the December 1992 economic summit in Little Rock, have visited the White House to discuss legislative packages with executive office personnel, and have testified before congressional committees.

On July 15, President Clinton sent the "Community Development Banking and Financial Institutions Act of 1993" to Congress, explicitly mentioning the South Shore Bank, among others, as the kind of institution he had in mind as a model for the program. This bill establishes a fund to make grants and loans of up to $5 million available to community development institutions, mainly on a matching dollar-for-dollar basis. The money will be issued for business development, neighborhood revitalization, and enhanced opportunities for low-income people as well as improved access to home ownership and rental housing for the same group. Sixty million dollars have been allocated for 1994, with projected increases to $111 million by 1997 and similar bills are being generated in Congress. The common thread in all of these legislative initiatives is the emphasis on fostering development by providing credit to low-income people.

Herein lies a fundamental problem. Shorebank's distinctive approach is derived from the discovery that providing credit alone is insufficient for solving the problems of low-income communities. Shorebank and its various spin-offs have demonstrated that an array of activities is necessary for generating quality credit demand and effecting productive change. In South Shore, aggressive real estate development by City Lands and The Neighborhood Institute created the conditions necessary for small investors to realize that real estate investment could actually produce a decent return. Credit then became a means to an end, not an end in itself. In South Arkansas and the upper peninsula of Michigan, experience has shown that a variety of activities are necessary just to stimulate demand for credit. This is not a world where large numbers of qualified credit-starved individuals are waiting in line. Consequently, a successful development program must be multipronged and proactive. With its emphasis on credit, President Clinton's bill does not pay sufficient attention to the additional elements.

Furthermore, President Clinton's legislation would require institutions to become self-sustaining in order to qualify for assistance. If the ultimate goal is real development—and not simply making loans to low-income people—such programs are likely to fail as long as "self-sustaining" is defined as an organization's ability to "earn its own way"—i.e., support itself by the profits it makes off loans, without some kind of continuing subsidy. In communities with large poor populations this model will be self-defeating. Their economies are not like perpetual motion machines that once set running will maintain themselves. Except where making loans to the poor is a peripheral activity of an ongoing financial institution, some subsidization will be necessary for such enterprises to succeed in the nonfinancial part of their task—providing technical assistance, leveraging economic activity through marketing and other programs, and providing other types of support that will allow loans to be productive.

Nonetheless, it is clear that as these legislative packages are designed, Shorebank and its many enterprises will be in an excellent position to receive federal funds. In addition, Shorebank's high-quality personnel can be counted on to deliver well-prepared proposals on time. This has already been illustrated in Arkansas, where a Southern subsidiary was the first organization in the country to receive funds from a new Small Business Administration Program designed to support microenterprises.

THE FUTURE

From one perspective the future of Shorebank and its affiliates and partners looks very bright. The company has made the transition from a relatively obscure and devoted little bank to an increasingly important American institution. The company operates efficiently and with a high level of integrity. It has attracted intelligent and energetic staff members with a genuine commitment to its mission. Its story epitomizes the American spirit: it emphasizes the importance of individual initiative in making a better life. Through credit, the bank provides the resources to make that happen. It would be a serious mistake to sell this management short. In a nation where poverty refuses to be vanquished and concentrated populations of poor people become threats to themselves and to the well-being of the larger society, any success story deserves the attention it gets.

Despite—or because of—the accolades, Shorebank faces potential problems that exist within the organization, in the communities it serves, and in the way it interacts with those communities.

Internal Challenges

Any student of management and organizational behavior must see warning signs in the rate of Shorebank's expansion. There are several types of management problems generated by rapid growth. The first is creating a management structure that does not require direct supervision of those at the top of the organizational hierarchy. There was a time not long ago when managers were shuffling on a regular basis between Chicago and Arkansas and between Chicago and Kansas City. Today, top managers spend much of their time meeting with officials in Washington and New York, with occasional trips to Eastern Europe, Bangladesh, and Pakistan. Add Marquette, Cleveland, and Willapa Bay to that itinerary and the difficulty of overseeing and managing the entire operation without structural change becomes obvious.

In a large and complicated organization, a good administrative structure will give reasonable autonomy to local managers who cannot be supervised closely and who are dealing with complex and novel environments requiring site-specific decisions and strategies if the organization is to be effective.

Once the proper structure is established, the second major challenge is to recruit people to manage the new endeavors. While Shorebank has hired talented staff, it has not had great success recruiting senior line managers. Recruiting is difficult because Shorebank has few other real-world counterparts. The combination of both tough-minded business skills and a commitment to social values that are not easily measured is not often found in a single individual. It is no accident that many of Shorebank's key personnel have not had formal business training.

Shorebank managers must also be able to manage risk and credit in an environment of federal regulations. Since few people meet all of these qualifications, some positions remain unfilled for long periods of time. Further, relatively autonomous managers must be imbued with an understanding and commitment to Shorebank's distinctive organizational style and goals. Indeed, there are already managers in this operation who are less committed to helping the poor or to doing site-specific development activities than is top management. A dangerous short-term solution would be to cannibalize Shorebank's existing operations to find staff for the new ones. Observers of the Arkansas enterprise are already expressing anxiety about losing valued staff as they hear about expansion plans.

The long-term solution is for the organization to grow its own managers. Until late 1993, Shorebank had no formal plan in place to do so; operating for so long with limited resources, it saw such a program as an unaffordable luxury. However, with the growth of capital and increased demand for its services, Shorebank management now hopes to implement an internal management training program. While current expansion plans necessitate short-term recruitment of managers from the outside, internal recruitment and training will have to become a more distinct part of the operation. Fortunately, because of Shorebank's increasing visibility, it is able to attract younger staff with a shared commitment to the organization's original goals.

External Challenges

The management challenges described above are an inevitable concomitant of growth. There are, however, problems in the environment that cannot be internally controlled. When I wrote this book, I suggested that one reason for Shorebank's success in South Shore was that the neighborhood was not extremely deteriorated. There was still good housing stock and the community itself maintained an underlying organizational structure. For example, community members organized themselves to abolish liquor sales in several precincts that contained trouble-producing bars and clubs. The community was also heterogeneous in terms of income level. Although one-quarter of the residents were below the poverty line, large numbers of people had steady jobs and substantial accomplishments on their records. The tools that Shorebank brought to this setting were appropriate for addressing the challenge of community revitalization.

However, life is getting objectively worse in many inner-city areas. The prevalence of unemployment, teen-age pregnancy, gang violence, and drug use may have broadened the gap between community needs and Shorebank's ability to meet them. For example, Shorebank and other organizations that develop inner-city housing find it increasingly difficult to maintain properties under these violent and unstable conditions. The resulting increase in management costs further compounds the problem.

In addition to maintaining physical properties, at least two additional concerns have to be addressed effectively if community development is going to succeed. One is the production of jobs. The Austin Labor Force Intermediary, combined with a good business development program, can begin to provide people with jobs and the belief that a structure of continuous employment is possible for those who work for it.

The second concern is the effort to identify strong elements in the community and help them organize, with the help of law enforcement agencies, schools, and social services, to combat disruptive elements and encourage productive activities—to a greater extent than Shorebank has so far accomplished. Originally, I identified Shorebank's ability to hold the community at arm's-length as one of the reasons for its success. At that time, community groups were wrangling over resources and approaches, and some elements, perceiving Shorebank as an unlimited supply, attempted to slow down the development process in hopes of being paid off to go away. Under those circumstances, the capacity to keep the community at a distance made sense.

Today, fewer low-income communities appear able to organize themselves for long-term productive behavior. Community organizations seem able to generate bursts of effort and then dissipate their initial accomplishments over the long, slow job of implementing a complex program. Lending institutions must work with other organizations to encourage the reconstruction of the social fabric so that the stable elements in the community can work together to achieve shared goals.

This is not to suggest that Shorebank should cease to do what it does well—rehabilitating housing and providing credit to those who need it and demonstrate that they will use it productively. But to the extent that it undertakes development activities in communities more severely deteriorated than South Shore, it may face insurmountable challenges. I should add that, although we are accustomed to thinking of these problems as distinctly urban, rural communities increasingly face such destructive influences as gangs, drugs, and crime.

Business Development

In addition to internal management problems and changes in the external environment, there is a third challenge to Shorebank programs. Shorebank and its constituent companies have yet to demonstrate that they can grow non real estate-related businesses in ways that benefit the poor, minority populations to a significant degree. Although almost every suborganization connected to Shorebank has some business development success stories to tell, the volume of achievement is still relatively small. In rural areas, the problem is tied to weak overall economies, where credit by itself cannot generate much business growth. In the urban sector, Shorebank's greatest successes come from real estate development. Many of the successful minority business people are landlords. With the wealth of experience generated from Chicago, Arkansas, and Michigan, and new interest in the use of incubators in Cleveland, it seems evident that Shorebank is moving toward effective business development. We have yet to see if these models will work.

CONCLUSION

Since the initial publication of *Community Capitalism*, the Shorebank organization has moved from obscurity to being defined as a major tool in the effort to reduce poverty, particularly through encouraging the achievements of local individuals. This approach is particularly important as U.S. policies at the federal level may result in the increased export of low-wage, unskilled jobs and the imperatives of global competition reduces the number of employees needed for any given level of output and investment.

Staffed by capable, energetic, and committed people, Shorebank has demonstrated a capacity to generate movement in a world where so many efforts are doomed to failure. Its foreseeable future challenges are in part the products of its own success, the fact that some kinds of community deterioration may outrun a single organization's ability to combat them, and the result of frustration generated by unreasonable expectations. How they got started and produced a viable, vital organization is the subject of this book. How they make use of new resources, public attention, and new opportunities for growth remains to be seen. Given the levels of accomplishment so far, one can be sure the experience will be significant.

Acknowledgments for the Paperback Edition

No organization likes to be under continuous scrutiny. Yet, in my relationship to Shorebank for more than twenty years, scrutinizer has been part of my role. By now the original founders of the company are old and good friends and accustomed to having me around.

But the company has grown enormously since those early days, and I have been unusually well positioned to observe new undertakings. This is particularly the case for Shorebank efforts in the Austin community in Chicago and in southern Arkansas. What is really striking is how open and helpful the new participants are. When things start out and optimism is high, everyone is eager to have a historian and friendly evaluator around. When things do not go well, as is inevitable in a learning experience, the temptation is to run for cover. Yet, even when the news seems not to be good, many Shorebank and Southern Development Corporation managers have been willing to share data with me and tell me their plans, hopes, and aspirations. This sometimes takes considerable personal courage. In the process of conducting business, many of these people have become friends. As friends, we fight sometimes, but their willingness to continue the relationship makes me grateful.

Similarly, two foundations, Ford and MacArthur, have made it possible to continue tracking some of Shorebank's and Southern's efforts. One reality of economic development programs is that they take a long time to bear fruit. To get a true assessment of what is being achieved, reasonably long time frames are required. Foundations are often unwilling to support slow long-term assessments, especially those that focus on the ongoing process. Again, because this sort of project takes a long time, there is the inevitable turnover of foundation personnel forced to carry on tasks initiated by others. For recipients of foundation support, these transitions can be difficult. Although everyone I have dealt with has been helpful, I wish to give special thanks to Roland Anglin, Lisa Mensah, Judith Samuelson, Frank DiGiovanni at Ford and to Paul Lingenfelter at MacArthur.

Acknowledgments

In 1973, Ronald Grzywinski invited me to observe his purchase of an inner-city bank and use of it as a vehicle to create economic development and community revitalization. I took him up on the offer, because the bank seemed unusual, and social scientists very seldom get to watch a project work itself out from the very beginning. To do so gives one the opportunity, in a way that hindsight seldom allows, to see roads not taken and choices made.

In the intervening years, three probability-sample surveys of South Shore residents were conducted, large quantities of other kinds of statistical and historical data were collected, and about seventy-five social science students at the University of Chicago had their first fieldwork experience in the South Shore community.

During that period, Mr. Grzywinski and his founding colleagues, Mary Houghton and Milton Davis, were unfailingly patient, kind, and helpful. It is difficult to thank them adequately. Other Illinois Neighborhood Development Corporation personnel, including Jim Fletcher, Jim Bringley, Michael Bennett, Tom Heagy, Tom Gallagher, George Surgeon (who started out as a fieldwork student and went on to be an INDC executive vice president), Paul Carson, Steve Perkins, Dorris Pickens, and David Oser, provided similar levels of assistance. Stan Hallett was also helpful. Richard Sander provided useful data. The list of other helpful IND personnel would more than fill this page.

Sara Lindholm started on this project as a research assistant and ultimately became president of one of INDC's affiliates. The high quality of much of the early data is due to her efforts. She also read the final manuscript and made numerous helpful suggestions.

Many students from the Department of Sociology worked on the project. Phyllis Betts's contribution is acknowledged within the book. Jan Dunham did fieldwork and read an early version of the manuscript. Stan Merrill did much preliminary statistical work. Alene Bycer organized and supervised one of the surveys. Joe Varacalli walked the streets of South Shore, counting shops and evaluating them. Tom Bonzar, Gus Schattenberg, Eric Hirsch, and Tony Babinec all played a role in the early days of the project.

And students from the undergraduate college at the University of Chicago satisfied their fieldwork requirement by doing research in South Shore as well. So many were involved that one observer remarked that just as African tribes knew they had arrived when an anthropologist decided to study them, South Shore community groups knew they were important when a University of Chicago student began to attend their meetings.

South Shore residents themselves were unfailingly helpful both to me and to the students, who often were uncertain about what they were doing. One by-product of the study was the opportunity to meet large numbers of truly outstanding individuals in the community.

Debra Sutherlin read an early version of the manuscript and made helpful suggestions, as did Robin Erickson. Both Monica Powell and Elaine Reardon provided editorial and production assistance. Elaine Reardon also produced the maps and the figures. David Osborne contributed useful organizational ideas.

The research was supported by the Wieboldt, Ford, Charles Stewart Mott, and Ernest Gallo foundations. Bob Johnson of the Wieboldt Foundation and Sol Chafkin of the Ford Foundation were particularly helpful in the early stages of the research, as was Professor George Rosen, who put me in touch with Chafkin. The Wieboldt, Joyce, Ford, and J. Roderick MacArthur foundations helped fund preparation of the book.

A research project is always a journey of adventure. This project particularly belongs in that category, because it marked a professional transition for me from student of India to student of America's cities. I am grateful to all of the above for assisting in that transition.

COMMUNITY
CAPITALISM

1

Introduction
The Illinois Neighborhood Development Corporation: A Bank Holding Company

The board of the Illinois Neighborhood Development Corporation (INDC) had assembled for its quarterly meeting in a downtown Chicago hotel.* It looked like the board of directors of any moderately prosperous company in 1986. Aside from the fact that the racial distribution between blacks and whites was more evenly balanced than it usually is at such meetings and that there were probably a few more women present than is normally the case, it could have been a board meeting anywhere.

The opening report on its operations sounded much like the report of any successful corporation. Clearly, the company, through its four subsidiaries, was having a good year. One would have guessed that this was always the case, as the directors nodded sagely with each report. The corporation's centerpiece was, indeed is, a bank, the South Shore Bank. Bank officials reported that if the year continued as it had been going, profits would be approximately $1,500,000, representing about 1½ percent on assets. These profits included a large write-off, and an increase in the bank's loan loss reserve. According to

*In 1986, the Illinois Neighborhood Development Corporation changed its name to the Shorebank Corporation. Because it was INDC for most of its life and because name changes are confusing, that is the name I give the corporation throughout the book.

the trade, a bank is doing fine if its profits are approximately 1 percent of assets. With about $100,000,000 of deposits, South Shore Bank was doing better than OK. In addition, although committed to doing most of its real estate lending within its own neighborhood, Chicago's South Shore, it had begun to make loans in a nearby neighborhood as well.

At a time when it seemed that extensive tax reform was in the wind, talk turned to what could be done about the large volume of taxes the bank would have to pay because of its profits.

City Lands Corporation (CLC), a real estate development company and another of the organization's subsidiaries, reported that it would earn about $125,000 in the coming year. It had finished or would finish the rehabilitation and construction of 63 units of housing, and had another complex planned. It was also working on a project for a mini–shopping center along the area's main commercial strip. The CLC president reported that the supermarket that was to be the unit's anchor tenant had decided that it needed more square feet than had originally been proposed.

The president of The Neighborhood Institute (TNI), a community service organization that was a third subsidiary (called, in this instance, an affiliate), reported that it would complete 67 units of housing by year end. TNI also held in hand about $600,000 worth of contracts for its job placement and general educational degree programs.

Corporation officials then talked about other plans and programs. The Federal Savings and Loan Insurance Corporation had just turned down the INDC's request to purchase a small, troubled savings and loan association in a California city. Plans were under way to extend the corporation's activities to a Chicago neighborhood on the other side of town, and personnel were being assigned. And both the governor of a southern state and the head of its largest foundation wanted the corporation to open a similar operation in their state. The foundation head had come to the meeting so that he and the board could get to know each other better. By the time the meeting was over, it seemed fairly certain that the corporation would open a branch in that state, with a big chunk of the initial investment coming from the foundation.

If one were to assume that this was the board of an ordinary but successful small corporation, none of these facts would be terribly startling.

But this was not an ordinary corporation. It was the Illinois Neighborhood Development Corporation (INDC), a peculiar hybrid company in the private sector, incorporating both profit-seeking and not-for-profit elements while committed to generating economic development in what had been a deteriorating neighborhood, South Shore, on Chicago's black South Side. (See Figure 1.1.) Its stockholders are not profit-seeking individuals, but foundations, religious groups, and moderately wealthy individuals concerned about the future of minorities in the nation's older cities. The company is organized as a for-profit bank holding company. As such, it must face the discipline of the marketplace and meet federal and state standards for banks and bank holding companies. The stockholders became participants in order to see if a banking organization could succeed where governments have failed: that is, in reversing the economic fortunes of a city neighborhood that had hit the skids. Their target was a community of approximately 75,000 residents, most of them black, that had undergone rapid racial and economic change in the mid-1960s. As so often happens, housing vacated by the middle class, first white and then black, became occupied by the poor, with disinvestment and deterioration following.

The question of whether a properly organized company, at least theoretically driven by the profit motive, could succeed in those neighborhoods that private for-profit actors have normally eschewed and where public moneys have not been notably successful in improving the environment, became for them simultaneously a theory to test and a challenge to meet. The stockholders had been willing to explore the proposition that a profit-seeking bank equipped with complementary additional subsidiaries, located in a more or less inner-city neighborhood, could have a substantial positive impact on the area *and* survive as well. In America of the 1970s and '80s, that

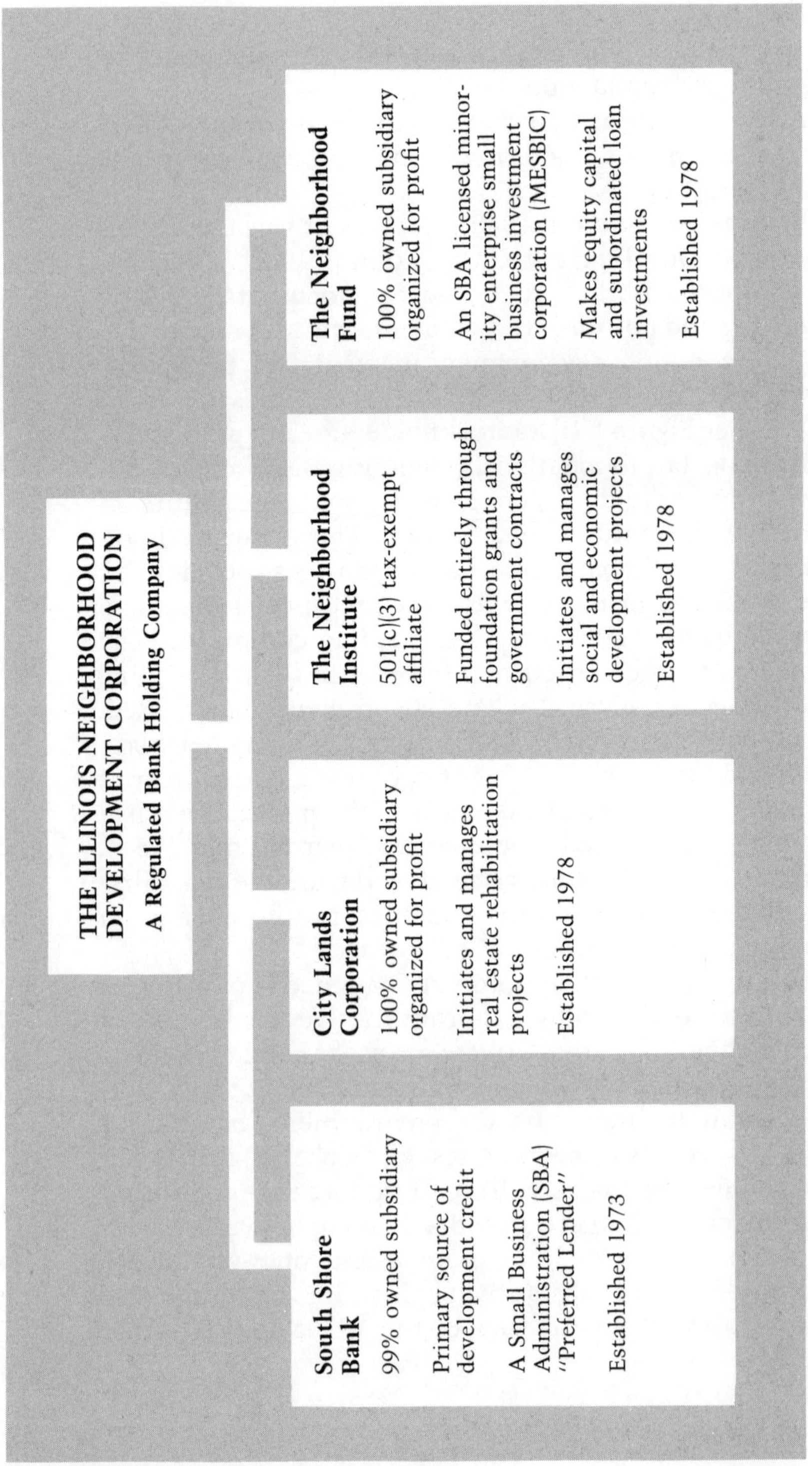

THE ILLINOIS NEIGHBORHOOD DEVELOPMENT CORPORATION

A Regulated Bank Holding Company

South Shore Bank

99% owned subsidiary

Primary source of development credit

A Small Business Administration (SBA) "Preferred Lender"

Established 1973

City Lands Corporation

100% owned subsidiary organized for profit

Initiates and manages real estate rehabilitation projects

Established 1978

The Neighborhood Institute

501(c)(3) tax-exempt affiliate

Funded entirely through foundation grants and government contracts

Initiates and manages social and economic development projects

Established 1978

The Neighborhood Fund

100% owned subsidiary organized for profit

An SBA licensed minority enterprise small business investment corporation (MESBIC)

Makes equity capital and subordinated loan investments

Established 1978

Figure 1.1   The Illinois Neighborhood Development Corporation

Source: The Woodstock Institute. "Evaluation of the Illinois Neighborhood Development Corporation." Used with permission.

proposition was so unlikely that only foundations and similarly committed individuals were apt to buy into it. That years
later the board would be discussing both a tax problem generated by large profits and the issue of paying off the preferred
stock purchased by some of the foundations is quite remark-
able. At a historic moment when deregulation had made the
banking business a perilous one, talk of such profits was even
more noteworthy. That the company's officers were willing
to duplicate—in fact, enthusiastic about duplicating—their
economic development activities in another inner-city neighborhood even further deteriorated than South Shore seems
still more astonishing.

What is clear is that the INDC is an uncommonly successful
inner-city development organization. What might not be clear
from the minutes of that board meeting is how difficult it was
to succeed, what an arduous and committed task it was for the
main actors, and how many mistakes they made along the way.
Even today, many of its achievements are fragile and will stand
and be consolidated only through substantial renewed effort.

The INDC has become a multipronged development instru-
ment with each of its subsidiaries—the South Shore Bank,
City Lands, The Neighborhood Institute, and The Neighborhood Fund—playing a distinctive and supporting part. The
result is an orchestrated effort in which each unit's output
serves to assist and support the output of the other units to
produce unusually high levels of economic growth for the
whole community. The structure of the organization itself,
then, and the way the parts relate to one another is worth
paying attention to.

The South Shore Bank is the centerpiece. It is situated to
generate resources and to invest in the community. City Lands
is a developer that mainly buys buildings, some of which have
been abandoned, and upgrades them for a profit. The Neighborhood Institute is a not-for-profit community organization that
works with community residents when they are threatened
by displacement by City Lands or bank development efforts,
provides job training and placement, is able to attract funds
for not-for-profit development activity, and has itself become

a major developer of housing. And The Neighborhood Fund, a minority enterprise small business investment corporation (MESBIC), provides venture capital through a Small Business Administration program for exciting and potentially profitable new business developments. Together, the components have become a formidable asset in the South Shore area.

A great deal has been written about urban economic development and the large sums of money spent to achieve it. Despite all the expenditure of effort, however, there is not much to show in measurable outcome. In contrast with most development agencies such as major national foundations and departments of city and federal government, INDC, with its small bank and relatively paltry resources, would appear to be an unpromising factor in urban revitalization. The fact that INDC is modestly successful in its effort makes it especially significant.

URBAN ECONOMIC DEVELOPMENT

Before we turn to the bank and its program, let me raise some general issues. Efforts at urban economic development are not news. Most big American cities are scarred or beautified by massive downtown projects designed to remove decayed structures and the low-income residents who live in them. The object is to replace both with dramatic modern buildings that house offices for prosperous service businesses, shops to attract the upper-middle class and apartments to house it, and, in some cases, through audacious planning, to bring tourists and conventions to town as well.

In addition to these big downtown projects, economic development in many cities also takes place by gentrifying residential areas. Young professionals with small households move into older areas that have been made attractive by pioneering "rehabbers" followed by developers and further buttressed by judicious use of urban renewal and other government incentive programs (see Taub, Taylor, and Dunham, 1984). Gentrification often drives out the poor who cannot pay the new high rents or the increased property taxes that result from neighborhood upgrading.

To be sure, big downtown projects do not always succeed—for every Boston there is a Detroit, and areas expected to gentrify sometimes do not—but nonetheless, these are the sorts of activities that characterize urban development in America.

These two development approaches, gentrification and downtown renewal, have several features in common. They benefit whites mainly (indeed, success is partly measured by the removal of minorities), they cater to the affluent, and they make use of resources provided by the higher reaches of city and federal governments to gain subsidies, powers of eminent domain, special zoning restrictions and easements, the closing of streets, and the location of new or improved public facilities, art centers, and hospitals.

Measures as dramatic as these are said to be necessary. Urban decay and other urban problems are so pervasive that only the greatest power and resources can surmount them.

These projects sometimes succeed on their own terms. There is another kind of urban development program that has been less successful. Designed to benefit the great ghettos of the North and West, the programs spend massive sums of money from major foundations and federal agencies to bring these communities back from slum status.

As a class, the programs have been notably unsuccessful. In many cases, the funds have disappeared without a trace, and in many of the other so-called more successful efforts, one could, in the words of one local leader, fly an airplane over the area before and after development and not perceive any difference. Where differences have been noticeable, it is often because local development corporations—that is, local community agencies created to encourage economic development—have behaved like the big downtown developers. They undertake large projects, which they construct on land assembled either by displacing the original residents or by waiting for (or hastening) the deterioration leading to abandonment.

Development programs at best produce, for the most part, the stuff of heartwarming anecdotes but very few measurable, positive results.

Neighborhood economic development is a little bit like brotherhood. All are in favor of it, but most often seem unwilling to take the steps necessary to do something about it. Part of its appeal is very much in the American populist tradition. Neighborhoods are where the little people live, and it is important that the little people get their fair share. For many, neighborhood economic development is often juxtaposed with downtown development. If the little people live in the neighborhoods, the big guys hang out downtown. Downtown is where national corporations have their headquarters, major department stores have their outlets, where the area's major financial institutions as well as the major real estate operators locate their primary activities.

The idea of neighborhoods often evokes sentiments of nostalgia and warmth. Tightly knit immigrant communities, which provided support to kin and fellow ethnics and where commercial streets carried exotic and specialized merchandise advertised in mysterious languages, are part of the idea of an urban neighborhood. Neighborhoods were and still are the staging ground for new Americans, who provided cheap labor in factories and construction projects and who operated small shops for long hours. The image also includes the idea that through education, immigrant offspring will enter the ranks of white-collar workers and professionals.

That same general orientation toward urban neighborhoods runs through the community of academic urban specialists as well. If we look through the historically important literature about urban neighborhoods or communities, we discover that the source of their theories is the study of urban ethnics. Indeed, most of the perspective-forming books have been about Italian, Jewish, and Polish neighborhoods.

Some dissonant realities intrude, however. A growing proportion of inner-city neighborhoods are the homes of racial minorities who often evoke more apprehension and less nostalgia than do their ethnic counterparts, either in the popular literature or among those who are paid to think about cities. We think in stereotypes. In the old ethnic community, there is the overweight woman shouting to her child from a third-floor window, threatening him with a beating when his father gets home. In the minority community, the stereotype includes no resident father, but there are men standing around on the street drinking from bottles in brown paper bags, frightening all who pass by (see Anderson; Hannerez; Liebow). (To be sure, in both the scholarly literature and in real life, things are more complicated. One of the major ethnographies about Italo-Americans concerns men, some of whom are Mafia-connected [Whyte], standing on the street corner. There is a paucity of literature, however, about non–street-corner black men—that is, those who stay with their families and hold jobs—although such men are clearly in the majority.)

Often areas of high crime and dramatic physical deterioration, these neighborhoods need something done to improve them physically and to ameliorate the lives of their residents. The two images of neighborhood—one ethnic and *gemütlich*, the other black and dangerous—do not blend very well. Indeed, much of the impetus for the national neighborhood movement has come from ethnic leaders who are trying to keep their neighborhoods from changing racially.

The same populist-generated interest in the neighborhoods, often blended with other concerns for the poor, leads to fear of displacement: that is, the removal of the poor to make way for the better-off. That concern generates greater moral outrage when the displaced are older people of ethnic stock who have lived in an area for some time than when they are younger minority group members who are also newcomers. In many actual cases, the rhetoric centers on the former while reality involves the latter.

For those trying to generate "development," the tension is obvious. It is difficult to produce physical improvement in an area without raising rents. And in some instances, with really poor tenants crowded into small areas with large numbers of inadequately supervised children, it is difficult to generate physical improvements of any sort. In those circumstances, how can neighborhood development ensure that current residents will be the prime beneficiaries? Those concerned about economic development, then, must walk a tightrope. On the one hand, they must encourage improvement of an area. On the other, they must not improve it enough to raise property values, for if they do, either renting tenants will be displaced as landlords try to collect the higher rents their improvements justify, or landowners will be forced out by the higher property taxes that are engendered by property appreciation.

Does neighborhood economic development mean driving out the poor and encouraging the presence of a new population or does it mean improving the life circumstances of the residents? A deteriorating neighborhood is one in which the physical structures are falling apart, and whose shopping strips have high vacancy rates or second-class uses such as fortune-telling and storefront churches. Consequently, economic development at the community or neighborhood level tends to focus on the improvement of those structures, the built environment. Expressions like *changing communities, bottoming out,* or *deteriorating* are either statements about buildings or statements about who is moving in or out. They are seldom statements about the lives of the residents.

I do not want to belabor this point. But to fail to understand it is to fail to understand much of what is important about the economic conditions of urban neighborhoods. For example, imagine a neighborhood economic development program that improved the earning opportunities of so many people that all of the able-bodied were able to move away. Those who remained would be the poorest and the most incapacitated and, consequently, unable to maintain the properties in the area. In this case, the economic development program for the area might be considered a failure. Yet a case can be made that such a program was a smashing success. Numerous residents' lives did improve.

This tension underscores one of the unexplored, almost unconscious issues of neighborhood economic development. The idea is built on a metaphor embracing the Marshall Plan after the Second World War, and efforts to promote economic development in third world countries after the dramatic success of American aid in Western Europe. Like much analogical thinking that does not transfer well to new settings, the economic development metaphor as applied to Europe and the third world does not fit the problems of urban communities and neighborhoods. First, the United States did not rebuild the nations of Western Europe; Europeans did it themselves with assistance from the United States—that is, the Europeans had substantial resources in human capital. Second, the European and third world nations are independent states, and their situation, consequently, is not comparable to urban communities or neighborhoods.

Many of the assumptions that apply to countries as a whole apply much less well to particular pieces of turf such as urban communities. When a nation is upgraded, one expects there to be some impact on some of its inhabitants. The word *development* in relation to third world countries conjures up pictures of industrialization, increased production of goods, and, among the more sophisticated, modern and mechanized agriculture. Accompanying this conception is the vaguer notion that increased production of goods will redound to almost everybody's benefit to some degree. Locating a new factory in a neighborhood, by contrast, may make life worse for the residents, many of whom may be driven away by noise, smells, and traffic. International boundaries are real barriers—rules governing currency, citizenship, and so forth discourage departure, and countries likely to be destinations often discourage immigration. It is easier, for example, for individuals to move or be moved from one area to another—down the block or across the street—than it is to change countries: to emigrate or to be exiled. Since the early 1960s, some northern cities in the United States have suffered net population losses of more than 25 percent. We understand intuitively that whatever the facts for domestic urban economic development, improving a nation's economic position does not include sending all of its residents somewhere else (although some nations, in an effort to improve their distribution of wealth, have tried to eradicate or expel some proportion of their wealthier merchant groups— particularly if they were ethnically distinct).

Another difference between third world and neighborhood development is that urban neighborhoods are so caught in webs of interdependency and have so little autonomous power that actions outside the community may be more important for the community's future than any taken within it. Urban communities or neighborhoods are parts of large and complex cities. They do not have their own governments, or even their own administrative apparatus. They cannot control their own police or schools, for example. Neither politically nor administratively independent, they are also seldom economically self-sufficient. Residents usually work elsewhere, and if there are businesses that provide jobs to local residents, they are often absentee-owned. Neighborhoods that have deteriorated, then, are often places where outsiders have discontinued investments and loans, the provision of first-class city services, and the promotion of property sales to individuals and corporations.

To be sure, cities, states, and nations are all interdependent. Nonetheless, the opportunities for autonomy are more severely circumscribed for urban neighborhoods than they are in the other cases.

In the face of strong external forces, it is difficult to understand just what an urban community can do by itself to make the lives of its residents better.

This digression is important for understanding the achievement of INDC. It has been able to change the behavior of individuals within the community *and* to change the orientations toward the community of those relevant actors who are outside it. Without the latter component, little real change would probably have taken place. It is often the normative preference of those who study urban neighborhoods to focus on what goes on inside them, either paying little attention to what takes place in the outside world or viewing outsiders as the enemy. In some instances, this focus leads to recommendations for bootstrap economics—the neighborhood should lift itself mainly by its own efforts—even to proposals for solar roof gardens and energy production, sweat-equity housing renovation, and the pooling of meager resources. In others, it leads to a sense of helplessness. Seldom does it focus on the creative ways to generate and use outside resources. That is one reason why successful attempts at neighborhood development are so rare.

It is that focus on the world outside the community that makes the INDC effort worthy of special attention. This book is a report on an unusually successful effort, which is, in its origins, substantially more modest in scope than most publicized efforts at development to date. So far, it has been more successful in achieving its goals than many downtown projects and most of the community-based ones. Unlike those projects that were public efforts making massive use of public and other not-for-profit resources, this effort is a business. And finally, the effort takes place in a mainly black community, one that, as it succeeds, is still mainly black. These facts make it notable, and worth calling attention to by themselves.

But the larger question is, What can we learn from the effort? It is true that our big cities increasingly fail to provide decent living conditions for their residents, particularly for the poor and the minorities who make up an increasing proportion of those residents. Despite the highly touted successes of downtown redevelopment and the colorful news stories about gentrified areas, it is clear that much of the area outside the downtowns is in decline, a decline that is costly in economic and social terms. If we can learn about successes in such situations, perhaps we can develop tools to reverse these destructive processes.

After ten years of struggle, the South Shore Bank is making record profits. Similarly, although it is by no means a sure thing (the forces encouraging deterioration never sleep), the community seems to be showing economic growth in hard times as well as good ones.

But the South Shore community was not and is not a passive wagon to be pulled along by INDC. Its residents have their own goals, and, on occasion, they have been willing to assert themselves. Sometimes they have done so in concert with INDC efforts. At other times they have done so in ways that run counter to short-range INDC plans.

Although I have referred to the community collectively, it is a mistake to think of it as a simple, homogeneous place. With a population of more than 75,000, it is a large community. If it were not within the city limits, it would be the sixth largest city in the state of Illinois. Its income range is enormous, with quintiles at both the top and bottom of Chicago's income distribution. The diversity of its housing stock introduces another level of complexity.

I have also discussed INDC as a unitary actor. But its board of directors and the officers of each of its subsidiaries represent a diverse group. White and black, cosmopolitan and local, highly educated and less so, they too often pull in somewhat different directions.

This is to be a prescriptive document. By carefully following the development of the South Shore enterprise, I intend to lay down some guidelines for others. It will not do simply to suggest that one should find a ghetto and start a bank, if one wants to achieve economic development. There have been ghettos and there have been banks, and they are often not made for each other. During the time when I observed efforts in South Shore, banks in three predominantly black neighborhoods collapsed, two of them on South Shore's borders. So, by exploring INDC's successes and failures, I will explain strategies and tactics that make sense. There are many reasons why investors might stay away from a neighborhood like South Shore. I will try to show how these real and imagined obstacles might be overcome.

In this context, INDC is interesting because it has been able, to an unusual degree, to bring to its community outside resources while generating positive development activities internally. To accomplish this was to reverse the process of disinvestment, which was set in motion when the community began to change racially in the mid-1960s. The point is that measurable achievement comes only with the introduction of measurable resources from outside the community. As we shall see, INDC has brought to South Shore stabilization and modest growth after a period of decline associated with the process of racial change. There have been improvements in housing stock and consequent property appreciation. INDC has accomplished this with acceptable levels of displacement. And, although it was not necessarily planned that way, the process moved at a slow enough pace so that individuals could adjust to changes and even take advantage of them. And the corporation has achieved this in a community located in a larger region, including the city of Chicago and the Calumet industrial area, that has been faced with declining economic fortunes as the huge steel industry has atrophied.

To be sure, not all external social forces have worked against South Shore. The neighborhood has certainly been the beneficiary of the broad social trends that produced an enlarged black middle class during the late 1960s and early 1970s. Nonetheless, the region of which South Shore is a part was in decline during this period, and attitudes toward communities undergoing racial change were also fixed in ways that were not to South Shore's advantage.

What INDC, then, has had to do is not only change patterns of behavior inside South Shore, but to change the way relevant agencies in South Shore's environment relate to the community. Because of the pattern of racial change taking place in South Shore, outsiders with the capacity to allocate resources to it were unlikely to do so. Part of the INDC achievement has been to alter that pattern so that the community could become a beneficiary of both private- and public-sector investments and, in general, of the delivery of better quality services from the city than such neighborhoods usually receive.

Let me now turn to the story. I will begin with a discussion of INDC and its principal actors. From there, I will shift to the community in which INDC has had to play its part. I will then turn again to INDC and its activities and show the impact they have had on the community. Finally, I will pull the material together to see what can be learned from the effort and applied elsewhere.

2

Creating the INDC

The INDC is in many respects the creation of one person, Ronald Grzywinski. On the basis of a superficial examination of his biography, it would be hard to imagine a less likely person to be the moving force behind an inner-city development bank. He grew up a Polish-American youth in the ethnocentric neighborhoods of steelworkers in the southeast corner of Chicago, a region where black people's houses are still burned if blacks try to move in. Grzywinski has spent virtually his entire life within five miles of South Shore. Only a stint in the army and a brief period of service in a far suburban bank took him away.

Grzywinski was not even trained as a banker. A graduate of Chicago's Loyola University, he began his career selling International Business Machine computers. From there, he went to work for a bank in Lockport, a small city southwest of Chicago. Having become president of that bank, he helped put together a deal to purchase an ailing bank in Hyde Park, a neighborhood that is the home of the University of Chicago and that was struggling to deal with racial change, white flight, and deterioration.

Grzywinski was plunged into a milieu of fervid activism. To begin with, this was the 1960s, a period of great social ferment. In addition, Hyde Park has always been the scene of intense community organization activity. This tendency was exacerbated not only by the historic moment, but also by the fact that the community was coming through a controversial urban renewal program organized and energized by the university.

In his characteristically open and low-key style, he made bank space available for community group meetings and plunged into organizational life himself. It was not long after he helped to put the Hyde Park Bank back on its feet that he was operating an urban development division that took as its commitment the lending of money to minority entrepreneurs.

That sounds less impressive today than it did in the 1960s, when such activity was still considered unsound. The program's success earned it and Grzywinski a certain measure of good repute. Because of its minority lending program, the bank was also able to attract government and private depositors who shared an interest in helping blacks become successful entrepreneurs.

As he built the development division, he found three colleagues to work with him. One was Milton Davis, a black graduate of Morehouse College, who was both an employee of the University of Chicago Business School and leader of the Chicago chapter of the Congress of Racial Equality (CORE). The second was Mary Houghton, a white graduate of Marquette and Johns Hopkins universities and a program officer for the Johnson Foundation. They were subsequently joined by Jim Fletcher, a black graduate of Northern Illinois University and an employee of the Midwest headquarters of the Office of Economic Opportunity (OEO). Like Grzywinski, Fletcher had grown up within five miles of South Shore. His house, however, had been located in the Ida B. Wells Homes, one of the earliest and best of the public housing projects in Chicago.

The important point to remember is that none of the key actors was trained as a banker nor did any follow an orthodox route to a banking career. Each of them had a range of career experiences before entering the banking world, and this range both gave them all a diversified view of the world and enhanced their ability to break with banking tradition. On the other hand, the fact that Grzywinski had worked his way up through a traditional bank that was part of a respected banking chain gave him credibility in the circumscribed world of bankers.

In 1971, Grzywinski took leave of the Hyde Park Bank and joined the Adlai Stevenson Institute at the University of Chicago. The Stevenson Institute served as a think tank for mature individuals who wanted a break in their careers in order to consider social issues. Grzywinski made use of that period to look into possibilities for a neighborhood development center. He found Michael Bennett, a black community organizer from Ohio, who was a student at the University of Chicago School of Social Service Administration, to help him. Out of that effort, an initial proposal evolved that contained many of the elements of the final Illinois Neighborhood Development Corporation.

That proposal included a housing management and construction firm; a limited-dividend housing corporation; a Minority Enterprise Small Business Investment Corporation (MESBIC); a neighborhood financial institution along the lines of a credit union; a not-for-profit institute to obtain foundation grants, conduct research, and provide job training and other social services; and a community organization to serve as an investment trust, which would provide a vehicle for neighborhood residents to participate in the development process. The residents would be expected to invest in the organization and increasingly play a controlling role in organizational decisions.

A key point here is that the initial plan, conceived in the "power to the people" period of the 1960s and early 1970s and developed with the help of a community organizer, foresaw a level of community involvement in participation and management that was never to be achieved.

Supported by outside funding, planning continued for two more years, and during that period, the idea of a credit union as a centerpiece was replaced by a bank whose role became more central to the process. This revision was possible because of a change in the law pertaining to bank holding companies. At the same time, the role of citizen participation was downplayed in the plan, as the bank evolved into an orthodox business organization. An orthodox bank, it was hoped, would look more attractive to investors and, furthermore, had the potential for becoming a stable, profitable resource base for other components of the development effort.

Having a bank rather than a credit union also had important tactical justifications. First, a bank is an institution that does not need to be explained. Second, a bank has important symbolic value. It stands for economic stability and fiduciary responsibility, both in the community and outside. It is automatically counted as worthy and sound as it brings with it the imprimatur of the federal government and the corporate world. Third, because people who do business in the community are likely to share their interests with bank officials, these officials are in a position to use that knowledge to direct and coordinate the allocation of resources. Fourth, to the extent that it succeeds, a bank automatically interfaces with a large segment of the community who come in to do business, to ask questions, and to collect money for local organizations. And, finally, although it may not always be believed to be operating in the best interests of the community, a bank, because of all its regulators, is trusted not to steal.

Grzywinski had demonstrated that he could take an ailing bank and bring it back to health. He had also demonstrated that he, with the help of Houghton, Davis, and Fletcher, could lend money to minority entrepreneurs. What neither he nor anyone else realized was that their entrepreneurial lending began at a particular historic moment when black businessmen were being invited to purchase franchises in the newly booming fast-food industry, and that the astonishing success of these loans made the practice appear easier than it in fact was.

Armed with a new proposal to purchase "an unknown bank of unknown size in an unspecified neighborhood," Grzywinski set out in 1972 to raise money. His success in doing so must be counted as a great achievement. He first raised $320,000 from two businessmen who were known for their concern with social problems. With the help of an activist, sociologist minister named Stan Hallett, who was associated with the Center for Community Change in Washington and the Center for Urban Affairs at Northwestern University, he raised subsequent funds from the United Church Board for Homeland Ministries and the Executive Council of the Episcopal Church. The Wieboldt Foundation in Chicago was an early investor; and Grzywinski, with the help of borrowed funds, invested approximately $100,000 himself. Further commitments were secured from two additional foundations, Ford and Joyce.

FINDING A COMMUNITY

The next problem was to find a community that seemed appropriate and that had a bank located near or within its boundaries. At about that time, the South Shore National Bank came on the market.

From the point of view of a local black activist named Al Raby, a friend of Grzywinski and leader in the Independent Voters of Illinois, this was the perfect opportunity. The South Shore community, in which the bank was located, was not yet in a terribly deteriorated condition, but it had definitely begun to slide in that direction. Housing stock was still in good shape; citizens still took pride in their homes and believed that they could improve things. Raby believed that for the group's initial effort, it would be a terrible mistake to tackle a really badly deteriorated, demoralized community. The level of resources required to turn that sort of community around seemed far beyond the reach of this yet untried and underfunded organization. He felt that the bank could not achieve much without citizens doing a great deal themselves, and in a really deteriorated community, that level of citizen participation might not be forthcoming.

I will discuss South Shore in greater detail in chapter 3. At this point, it is sufficient to report that the South Shore community had begun the process of racial change in the early 1960s and had a population that was about 80 percent black at the time when Grzywinski was looking at it. An older community, it was in the course of decline and deterioration, which had begun before racial change and had, as is often the case, been augmented by the change process itself: white flight, a diminishing of city services, and ownership and some mismanagement of buildings by absentee landlords. There was, however, still extensive housing stock in good condition, and numerous property owners demonstrated that they had not given up by maintaining their buildings at a decent level, by participating in community organizational life, and by working at general maintenance of the area.

Grzywinski, Davis (who was one of the earlier black South Shore residents), and Raby hiked through the community, looking in alleyways and backyards, assessing both the community's infrastructure and resident attitudes toward it. The number of relatively clean and well-maintained areas convinced them that South Shore was indeed the place.

Although complex negotiations surrounded the purchase and the determination of its price, in August 1973, the bank was finally sold to INDC for $3.2 million—$800,000 in firm investment commitments, and a $2.4 million loan, guaranteed by Grzywinski and his wife, from the American National Bank.

The brute facts of the purchase underscore two aspects of South Shore Bank activities that will continue to be relevant for our analysis. The first is that INDC began life with a heavy debt load, whose weight handicapped INDC's performance for most of its not-yet-very-long life. Some observers are convinced that the size of that initial debt is the major reason why the bank took so much time to become really profitable.

The second, the personal loan guarantee, is important for understanding the success of the bank. Money lent with personal guarantees makes sure that people lose a great deal if they fail. This fact leads borrowers to work extra hard to make projects succeed, including, if necessary, sleepless nights and restless weekends. Very few great achievements happen in the framework of the forty-hour week. In the case of the South Shore bank, it meant that the new owners could not be part-time do-gooders. They had to make money. In addition, that personal stake demonstrated graphically to potential investors that management intended to succeed, had a reasonable chance of doing so, and would treat other investors' resources as if they were their own. It was just that kind of incentive that became a part of the bank's policy: requiring a personal guarantee from its loan applicants.

FROM PROPOSAL TO REALITY

With the purchase of the bank, the years of planning at last paid off. INDC came into being, and it owned a bank—not such a great bank, it is true, but a bank nonetheless. It was a bank in good shape in terms of liquidity, but one without much promise. It had suffered a $40 million decline in deposits over the preceding ten years, and many informed observers were sure that the outflow would continue and that the community did not have enough resources to support a bank. The physical structure of the bank had weathered a certain measure of deferred maintenance as resources were husbanded for a profitable sale. Its standing in the community was low, because it was widely perceived to be inhospitable to new residents—it was open during relatively few hours, paid low rates of interest, and was not making loans in the community. Finally, it began life supporting INDC's debt of $2.4 million pegged at the prime rate. There was much ground to make up.

At the time, the original plan to set up other related companies was deferred, and total effort went into making the bank a paying business and, simultaneously, toward beginning to move into development activities. This second point is worth keeping in mind. Although the bank was not positioned to operate successfully as a bank (as compared to being ready for sale), its officers made the decision to begin development activities immediately. The temptation in such a situation, and, it should be added, the suggestion of some graying heads in the banking world, was to wait before trying the unorthodox. If they had wanted to, bank officials could have postponed the development component of their efforts for some time, and that postponement would have been seen as prudent. But bank officials and their aggressive board felt that INDC was and should be primarily a development organization, and consequently they were unwilling to accept postponement to a more appropriate but undefined date. They felt that postponement would make them unproductively similar to other banks. Traditionally, the justification of other banks for not lending in a neighborhood revolved around their responsibilities to their investors and the danger of letting them down by taking risks—which, from the INDC management point of view, was operationally defined as not lending to minorities and, above all, not lending in minority neighborhoods. That was a road to be avoided.

Needless to say, this was a simplification. As part of a nationwide banking system, the bank had to meet certain standards in its economic performance. Periodic state and federal inspections were not trivial. Furthermore, representatives of American National Bank, who had made the large original loan, sat on the board and watched bank activities carefully in order to protect their commitment. Nonetheless, if the bank failed to produce a program of development activities, it would also fail to achieve the goals of board members and investors. When confronted at one meeting by the choice of a development alternative or waiting for better times, one of the directors asserted, "If we are to go down, we should go down in flames. We said we are a development bank, and we have to give that our best shot. There can be no other justification for our existence."

A successful development effort did not necessarily mean the long-run sacrifice of profitability. Part of the bank's development ideology includes the belief that as the community becomes more prosperous, so does the bank. And a prosperous bank might encourage other bankers to follow a similar route. Among some of INDC's early leaders, such an idea became even more extreme: INDC would purchase property and generate land banks. As the area became more desirable, this land could be sold for substantial profits. A program to accomplish this never did get under way—a good thing for INDC, for, although discernible, property appreciation for multifamily dwellings in South Shore was modest throughout the 1970s and would not have justified the initial investment.

The tension between profitability and development activity was, and indeed still is, ever present. And in time, definitions of development changed to accommodate the pressures from the external world. Nonetheless, it is crucial for understanding the future of INDC to realize that its commitment to development activity was and has been unwavering.

NEW MANAGEMENT

In August 1973, the South Shore National Bank changed hands. Its new management, Grzywinski, Davis, Houghton, and Hallett, took over an operating bank with deposits of about $38 million, a conservative staff, including a group of vice presidents who had served the old management, and a reputation for not being very helpful to the new members of the community.

For the new management and for some community leaders, it was a high moment. I remember visiting, as an observer, a South Shore community organization fund-raising event in September 1973, at which Grzywinski was present. People were nudging each other and pointing excitedly at the bank's new owner. The purchase of the bank did have some of the symbolic value for the community that the purchasers wished it would—it showed community members that an important fount of significant resources had not dried up; the community was not abandoned.

The representatives of the old management who had stayed on viewed the change either with dread and disappointment (to make the purchase possible, the bank had to reduce its capital, and therefore its standing in the banking world) or with a wait-and-see attitude. They had all followed orthodox business and banking careers. One came to the South Shore Bank fresh from college and had remained for twenty-five years. Another began as a loan officer in a lending company and shifted to the bank, where he had served for twenty years. A third came after a career as a bank examiner. It is both to their credit and that of the bank that, although they had marked differences in philosophy, all three top managers stayed on for several years after the bank changed hands. Having since departed for greener pastures, two of the three have continued to maintain relationships with the bank, including the exchange of business information.

Nevertheless, the first two years were characterized by a kind of duality in the management of the bank. The old-timers, with some assistance from Milton Davis, were supposed to run the bank and make it profitable, while the new management, led by Mary Houghton, was supposed to do development. That, of course, is too simple. In the early days, Mary Houghton studied important bank systems, such as setting up new accounts, and simplified them a great deal in order to make them more accessible. Milton Davis visited groups of local businessmen and encouraged them to take loans.

At that time, the achievement of profitability did not seem as if it would be a difficult task. One South Shore resident, a banker in a nearby suburban bank, believed that becoming profitable would be easy. With the Illinois prohibition against branch banking and the complex of regulations governing the function of banks in those preregulation days, he thought that a bank charter was a "license to make money." All that had to be done was to open the doors and smile, and customers and, consequently, income would come pouring in. The old South Shore Bank kept old-fashioned, short hours—particularly inappropriate when so many of the adults in the new South Shore families held jobs and could not get to the bank after 9:00 A.M. and before 2:00 P.M. on weekdays—and the staff seldom smiled at their new black customers. The new management planned changes to include more account options, longer hours, and a more welcoming orientation to attract customers.

Generating business was not very exciting for people whose goal was to revitalize the economic life of the South Shore community. The newcomers wanted mainly to do development. Indeed, rather quickly an informal caste system grew up involving the cosmopolitan types, who focused on the development effort, and the local folks, who took responsibility for the dreary business of running a bank. One bright young observer who came to the bank as an intern distinguished the "knowers"—those who made plans for development activities—from the "nonknowers"—those who looked after the bank's day-to-day operations. It is an important distinction to make, because with so much of the talent focused on development, it was a long time before management devoted sufficient attention to making the bank the profitable operation it was to become eight or nine years later.

That duality was heightened by the fact that it was not clear what it meant to make a development contribution in South Shore, or even how to make the bank an economic success. There was a general understanding that if the bank succeeded at development, the residents of South Shore would be better off: that there would be improved incomes and appreciation of property values, which would also lead ultimately to the bank's economic success. Development activity and banking success, however, often became bound up together in unanticipated ways. Indeed, one of the early conceptions of the bank's mission was that by the very act of providing comprehensive banking to people often normally denied it, the bank was achieving economic development. How that process worked, in fact, is a story yet to tell.

Before we consider that, however, let me turn to the South Shore community itself, for without a clear picture of the area in which INDC conducted its affairs, it will not be possible to understand fully the rest of the story.

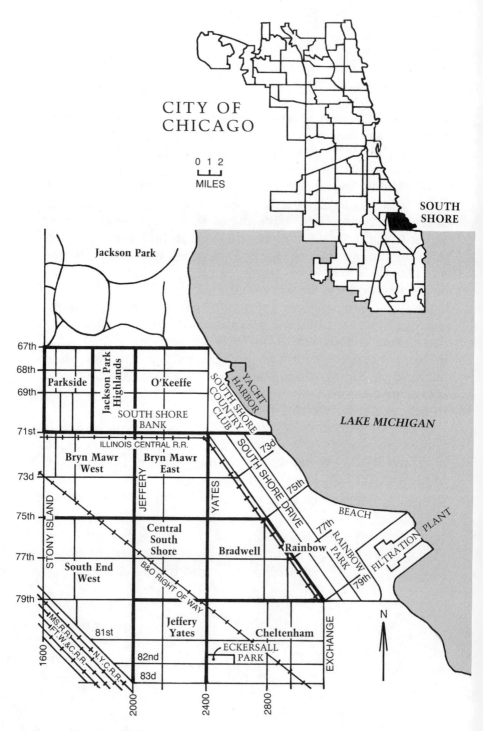

Figure 3.1   South Shore

3

The South Shore Community

The community called South Shore is located on the shore of
Lake Michigan nine miles south of the Loop, Chicago's central
business district. (See Figure 3.1.) It is connected to the downtown by a broad limited-access parkway, which runs along
the coast, a bus service that runs along the parkway, and a
commuter train that follows the same route.

The area is seven by twelve blocks square (eight blocks to
the mile) and has a population of about 75,000. In the 1920s,
a Chicago sociologist identified and labeled 75 community
areas, and today, although the city uses the old maps for various
planning purposes, there is some variation in the present use-
fulness of those labels. The present South Shore, however, fits
the old definition quite closely. Its western boundary has been
moved a few blocks eastward, the boundary street, Stony Island
Avenue, being an eight-lane city road. The northern boundary
is the large Jackson Park, which forms a ribbon running from
the lake to Stony Island. Sixty-seventh Street runs along the
southern edge of the park (the northern edge of the community). The eastern boundary, obviously, is the lake. The
southern boundary stretches from Seventy-ninth Street down
to Eighty-third Street. Just south of there, the now defunct
United States Steel South Works begins, hugging the lake shore
for another mile.

With its northern boundary a large and lovely park and its eastern boundary of lakefront and beach, South Shore has a lot going for it. For many years it was a residential community of some distinction. Created initially to house railroad workers during the Columbian Exposition in 1893, it became a solid middle-class bedroom community fairly rapidly. Its range of housing stock is unusually large. Single-family houses include the mansions of Jackson Park Highlands (South Shore is divided into a number of subneighborhoods), the solid houses of Bryn Mawr East, the small brick bungalows of Jeffrey-Yates, and the small frame cottages near the steel mills in Cheltenham. There is a similar variety in multiple-family dwellings. There are the solid old Chicago three- and six-flat buildings with large "railroad-style" apartments. There are U-shaped, three-story, courtyard buildings, large, square multiple-family dwellings, often with shops on the ground floor, huge grand old apartment buildings with marble lobbies and ornate exteriors, and, finally, along the lakefront, modern high rises of poured concrete and curtain walls.

At present, the variety of buildings is illustrative of the range of life-styles and classes in the community. The Highlands is the home of University of Chicago doctors and professors, important black professionals as well as such celebrities as Jesse Jackson and Ramsey Lewis. Some of the old walk-up buildings house welfare mothers, single men who have no visible means of support, and other members of the poverty class. In between, there are some professional singles and couples along the lakefront, the solid two-earner families—he a bus driver, a postman; she a teacher or a nurse—and other members of the middle class. The population is almost all black. There are a few elderly whites left in the community, although their number is dwindling, and a few successful white professionals in the areas with larger houses.

People remember the old South Shore wistfully. It was clearly a middle-class area. It is often alleged that the housing heterogeneity made possible intergenerational continuity as families in different life stages could find suitable housing within the community. Many of the residents were politically well connected in the late Mayor Daley's far-flung organization. The more northerly segments of the community consisted of substantial numbers of people of both Jewish and Irish backgrounds. They seem to have had little to do with each other, but to have gotten along all right. The center of this region is marked by a large Roman Catholic church, which used to be particularly influential within the archdiocese, its pastor a figure to be reckoned with. The very same area was dotted with smaller, yet quite distinctive, synagogues.

A jewel in the crown of South Shore was the South Shore Country Club. On the lakefront, it included a golf course, riding stables, bridle paths and a riding ring, a beach with a beach house, and clay-surfaced tennis courts. The clubhouse had elegant ballrooms and a dining room, ceilings held up by marble columns, and floor-to-ceiling windows looking out toward the lake. It was an exclusive place. Minorities, including the Jews who composed a substantial element of the South Shore population, were excluded from membership.

Ethnically speaking, there were other groups as well in South Shore. Toward the southern edge there was a large Swedish community, which supported some Lutheran and Baptist churches. Closer to the steel mills was a Polish population, its church dominating the center of its area. Seventy-first Street was the main shopping strip in the area, and the principal upper-middle-class shopping area for the whole southeast quadrant of the city. Despite the fact (or perhaps because of it) that the Illinois Central Railroad's tracks run down its center, today making it an unattractive street, it was lined with expensive stores, which at present, when they are found in the city, are on the fancy streets downtown. Expensive jewelers, furriers, deluxe shoe and clothing shops were all there, as well as myriads of beauty salons.

Its high school consistently ranked high in the city and sent its graduates to the best colleges. Some of its elementary schools were also among the highest-scoring in the city.

One knowledgeable social scientist said that the South Shore displayed "advantages that cannot be duplicated in the aggregate in any other community." He went on to say:

The South Shore is a community where the folly of the practice of migrating from older neighborhoods to new ones every generation can be strikingly demonstrated. There is no second South Shore lying along the lake front just beyond this community. A new residential area on the periphery of Chicago would be far from the cooling breezes, bathing beaches and yachting on the lake and it would be a long way from the great parks, shopping centers and the frequent and quick transportation to the Loop (Hoyt, p. 43).

It is difficult to make generalizations about the quality of social life. Many former residents remember it as a tightly knit community, at least for those in one of the major ethnic groups. On the other hand, one lifetime resident disputed that view. He said that it was the sort of neighborhood where people left each other alone. "It was the kind of place," he said, "where if you happened to see a fire engine heading down your street, and observed that it stopped in front of your neighbor's house instead of your own, you would breathe a sigh of relief and walk on."

In the 1950s, the community began to experience what might best be characterized as subtle decline. Many of the older buildings had been undermaintained during the Second World War and were now old-fashioned for those able to choose between living in South Shore and some of the great new buildings at the city's fringe or in the newly expanding suburbs. One informant reports going apartment hunting and being shown units with bathtubs with feet, which to him were outmoded and unacceptable. The community seemed to be undergoing the natural life cycle of many urban communities: as the housing became old and unfashionable, people moved on to newer and greener fields.

The process of decline was hastened by the threat of racial change. Woodlawn, to the north and west, had, by the late 1950s, become a largely black community. Hyde Park, a little farther north, was undergoing a large black in-migration. The combination of outmoded housing and the threat of the arrival of a minority population made the community less attractive to its traditional white middle-class occupants, and property values, increasing elsewhere, began to stagnate. Seeing the handwriting on the wall, citizens began to come together to decide how to deal with the new black residents. Out of these concerns, the South Shore Commission, a community organization, was born. Harvey Molotch (1972) documents this period rather well.

Initially, the commission was pulled between those who wanted to figure out how to keep blacks out of the community and those who wanted to keep whites in it. Efforts were made to make the community more attractive to existing residents. Leaders fought to get a new high school built (it eventually was, and in 1984 appeared on national television as a typical and really bad city school). With the help of the mayor, residents got the country club, whose membership was declining anyway, to admit Jews. A magnet elementary school was constructed, and there was an extra push for city services.

Finally, the commission tried to control access to housing as a way of either excluding blacks or preventing resegregation, depending on one's point of view. Of course, as Molotch points out, many things that were to make South Shore attractive to whites also made it attractive to the black middle classes, who had a smaller range of choices about where to live. In addition, there were large social forces driving low-income blacks into the community. For example, the gang problem in Woodlawn became quite severe as the famous Blackstone Rangers took control and Woodlawn began to deteriorate severely.

In Hyde Park, the University of Chicago presided over an urban renewal program that drove low-income blacks out of the community; some of them moved to South Shore. Black people were moving into the community then at two levels. Middle-class people took advantage of the availability of a whole range of quality housing. The poor began to move into some of the larger older units, which had been undermaintained and were now ripe for subdivision.

Efforts by the commission to control the rate, timing, and spatial location of racial change had little effect. The black population increased, and by the mid-1960s racial tensions began to affect the community.

Although change in general was fairly rapid, there were white families scattered throughout the community who chose not to move. Some of them continued to provide community leadership until the day they moved away. Others are still there. This community organizational structure into which the new residents could filter was important for South Shore. And, although ongoing arrangements are not terribly strong, the community has been able to mobilize for bursts of activity when they have been called for.

Throughout this period, the South Shore Commission has played an important role. In its early days, it was perceived by many as an organization formed to keep blacks out. When black membership began to grow, it came from those middle-class groups who wanted either to keep poor black people out or to drive them away. Indeed, there was often tension between the paid staff members and the leadership of the commission. Coming out of a tradition of community organizing, and particularly articulate about the problems of the black poor, the staff members instinctively turned for resources to those government agencies and private foundations whose orientation was to help the poverty class.

Similarly, they tended to articulate South Shore's problems as those related to problems of poverty. The leadership of the commission wanted the money, but it did not want to advertise the community as poverty-ridden. Tension about how to characterize the community persists to the present day. I have been criticized for using words like *inner city* or *ghetto* to describe the area. This ambivalence has been one of the reasons why the community has never been able to organize in a dramatic and systematic way. I will return to this topic later in this chapter.

When INDC purchased the bank in August of 1973, it found the community playing out the last act in the process of racial change. The community had a shadowy organizational structure, which included the South Shore Commission and eleven neighborhood organizations, each representing an area within the community that had enough reality to have a name.

The main shopping strip was in dramatic decline, with only a few of the old expensive clothing stores barely hanging on. A survey of storefronts in the area disclosed a vacancy rate of about 20 percent, and many of the stores still operating could no longer be reasonably considered deluxe. A systematic rating of those stores showed about one-third to be well maintained and two-thirds to be dilapidated.

Crime rates, which had been low, had soared to among the highest in the city. Index crimes were 83.7 per thousand, compared to 37.7 for the city as a whole.

Property values had also stalled. We compared the change in median sale prices, starting in 1960, for single-family houses in South Shore with two communities whose income and housing price levels were very similar. By 1974, South Shore housing prices had increased by 31 percent in nominal dollars, while the other two communities had increased by 98 and 134 percent, respectively.

Tax delinquency rates were climbing steadily in some of the more rundown areas of the community as well. The proportion of the population on welfare had risen to 23 percent, which was 10 points higher than for the city of Chicago as a whole. School test scores were moving lower.

The process of racial change was largely complete, with 85.6 percent of the population black. Our 1974 NORC survey showed that almost 24 percent of the households were single-person households and a similar proportion were headed by females.

As for religious breakdown, 69 percent of the population was Protestant, 17.6 percent was Catholic, 2.4 percent Jewish, and 1 percent Muslim. As might be expected in this mostly black community, among the Protestants, Baptists predominated.

About half the respondents had been born in the South, with 42 percent hailing from Illinois. Two-thirds reported urban backgrounds.

In terms of the socioeconomic standing of its members, the community reflected the diversity of its housing stock. There are large proportions at both ends of the scale. In a survey conducted eight months after the bank was purchased, 23 percent of the respondents reported family income as under $6,000. Thirteen percent reported family incomes in excess of $20,000, with another 7 percent in the $17,500 to $20,000 range. Four percent of the population reported family income over $30,000.

Reflecting the community's rapid change, most of the residents were new arrivals. Fifteen percent of the respondents had moved into South Shore in 1974, the year of the survey; 54.5 percent had moved into South Shore between 1971 and 1974.

Such rapid change was obviously disruptive. Rapid social movement into and out of a community contributes to that community's sense of disorganization, helplessness, and inability to police itself. Who are one's neighbors? Does that youngster standing on the street belong here? Whom can you get to look after your house if you are away for a few days?

In response to the question "How often do you spend a social evening with one of your neighbors?" half the respondents said they never had done so. Almost 19 percent reported that they did so once a week or more. Those, of course, were the older residents. More than half the respondents said there were no South Shore residents at all with whom they spent a social evening at least once a month.

Since most of the dwelling units in South Shore were apartments, and South Shore was slow to move into condominiums, 80 percent of all our respondents were renters.

As a way of discerning the attractions of South Shore at that time, we asked respondents to "Think back to when you first moved to South Shore. How important was each of these in your decision to move into South Shore?" We then listed a series of attributes which are shown in Table 3.1. Respondents were to choose their ratings on a five-point scale running from extremely important to not at all important. For purposes of clarity, we combine "extremely important" and "very important," and report the judgments in rank order.

Four items stand out on this list: safety, general appearance of the area, convenient shopping, and quality of police and fire

Table 3.1

*Percent Selecting Neighborhood Qualities as Reasons
to Move to South Shore*

Quality	Percent
Safety	89.6
Quality housing for the money	88.7
General appearance of the area	78.8
Convenient shopping	78.0
Quality of police and fire protection	70.4
Parks and recreation facilities	48.2
Traffic on the streets	47.8
Quality of public schools	41.5
Convenience to place of work	35.7
Neighbors with same background	31.9
Property taxes	22.3

protection. Each in its own way provides a kind of inverse image of the places from which most of these respondents came. Having fled, for the most part, from areas in decay and rife with gangs, respondents gave special significance to safety and police and fire protection. A walk through Woodlawn, Englewood, or North Kenwood, nearby neighborhoods in more advanced stages of deterioration at that time, would show burned-out houses, gang graffiti, and litter-strewn vacant lots.

Our survey also points to the general appearance of the area as an important category. Indeed, that particular item deserves a more extended comment because as I conducted the research, its high rank came as a surprise to me.

Let me start with an extended anecdote. One Sunday morning in another Chicago neighborhood, there was a fourteen- or fifteen-year-old black female adolescent standing at a bus stop adjacent to a large low-equity cooperative apartment complex. She became bored and, to kill time, began hanging on the branch of a small tree close to the stop. A short while later, an elderly black man and his wife leaving the complex passed by, presumably on their way to church. The woman was all dressed up and wearing a hat with flowers on top. The man was in a brown suit and wore a Panama hat. As they walked past the bus stop, they looked at the youngster, but kept on, glancing backward from time to time.

Suddenly, the man turned, leaving his wife halfway down the next block. He strode back to the youngster, and confronting her almost nose to nose, he said (approximately), "Young lady. Why is it that everywhere we move turns to shit? I will tell you why. Because young and careless and destructive and stupid people like you destroy everything that is nice. That tree is a young and brand-new tree. Your mommy and daddy own that tree, my wife and I own that tree. And you are tearing it down." He continued ranting for some time. She let go of the tree and looked at him sullenly. Obviously still agitated, he went back to his wife. They took two steps, and then he left her again. This time he returned to the building and found a security guard, whom he brought to the bus stop. The security guard took the girl's name, scolded her a bit, and told her that he would report the incident to her parents. The old gentleman, mollified, strode back to his wife, and they marched on down the street to church.

The story needs little elaboration. An attractive neighborhood means a great deal to people who find it difficult to find one, to say nothing of keeping it that way. It is the fight of the respectable to maintain order in a world that does not provide it easily.

Another anecdote. A group of people connected to South Shore are meeting downtown with another group who might spend money on that neighborhood. As president of the South Shore Commission, Raymond Davis represents the community. One person starts discussing infrastructure. Davis cautions him. "Whatever we spend money on," he says, "has got to show. That is what people want." He is chided for being superficial, yet his assertion is important evidence for the value of community input. In the light of our survey data, one can see why appearance is so important.

We then asked respondents how satisfied they were with those elements. Below in Table 3.2 appears a rank order of satisfaction with the categories "very satisfied" and "somewhat satisfied" combined.

Table 3.2

*Percent of Inhabitants Expressing Satisfaction
with Neighborhood Attributes*

Attribute	Percent
Convenience to employment	71.9
Convenient shopping	66.8
Traffic on the streets	57.9
Police and fire protection	56.0
Parks and recreation	55.3
Quality of housing	51.4
General appearance	51.2
Kinds of people	49.4
Safety	42.4
Public schools	24.5
Property taxes	10.2

If we juxtapose Tables 3.1 and 3.2 and if we make the some-what warranted assumption that the differences between the neighborhood qualities they thought they were getting and those attributes they now had were evidence of disappoint-ment, we can see that the community had not lived up to expectations. The four areas listed as most important for the move are not the ones that provide the most satisfaction now. In fact, about 20 percent of the population are disappointed by what they now have in these areas. This is not just general fussiness on the part of respondents. Indeed, there are some items they are quite contented with, such as convenience to place of employment. However, those dimensions did not rep-resent the most important reasons for choosing their commu-nity.

Too much cannot be made of these numbers. A person may be disappointed in some aspect of community life, but may decide that some other aspect more than compensates. In other research, we have observed that some kinds of perceived com-pensations can make up, for example, for unsatisfactory crime rates (Taub, Taylor, and Dunham, 1984). They never do, how-ever, when good housing value is not an important source of satisfaction. In South Shore, satisfaction with housing value is one attribute that displays substantial decline.

This finding fits with our field worker reports that South Shore was a somewhat depressed community. After their move, residents felt let down by developments. There was also an inverse relationship between length of residence and feelings of satisfaction. The longer a person had lived in South Shore, the more likely he or she was to feel that the neighborhood had declined. That was an accurate view of matters. Certainly, crime rates, welfare rates, and tax delinquencies had all soared within a relatively short period of time.

COMMUNITY ORGANIZATIONS

Although depressed in 1974 about the way things were going, community residents still included a certain number of activists. Although it was almost moribund, there was the skeletal structure of many community organizations, a few of which had maintained a measurable level of activity.

To begin with, there was still the South Shore Commission. It met regularly and had a twenty-three-member executive board of directors elected from subareas within the community. It no longer had enough money to pay an executive director, and it was operating in the red. But it still maintained an office where citizens could get information about the community and was about to hire an executive director, a community organizer who would be responsible for raising his own salary. The orientation of the board was upper-middle-class, and its most visible members came from the most prosperous areas of the community.

Each of the eleven subareas had some kind of organizational life. In two cases, Jackson Park Highlands and Bryn Mawr East, the two most prosperous areas of the community and the ones filled with single-family houses, the associations were indeed active—keeping an eye out for code enforcement, having parties so that residents could get to know one another, meeting with the police to encourage good levels of protection. Two more groups had clear organizational identities. Others met sporadically in response to crises. Although the whole community had only small numbers of white members, the commission and the two active area councils included substantial numbers of involved whites.

There was also a chamber of commerce in South Shore, made up of local businessmen. It limped along with chronic shortages of funds and small turnouts for its meetings.

Finally, there was the South Shore open-house committee, a group of women who organized an annual house tour of the area so that outsiders could see what a nice place South Shore was to live in, and insiders could gain confidence in the community and be in less of a hurry to leave. The committee was successful in that the open-house day attracted large crowds, and buses carried people from one carefully groomed house to another. Although the crowds for the open-house day exceeded the organization's capacity to handle them, it was less successful in its aims than it planned to be. Most of the tourers were South Shore residents who wanted to see how others lived. The committee also had developed a peculiar negative tradition. For each of the preceding three years, the person chosen to be president left the community shortly after her term of office was over. At the time of the INDC transition, the president of the open-house committee told us that she was determined not to leave. She wanted to break the chain.

As I suggested earlier, the community was able to mobilize itself, or, at least, some elements within it. The first big issue came in 1972 with the effort to keep the bank in the community, when its owners, certain that it could not survive the period of racial change, petitioned to move the license to a downtown location on the grounds that South Shore's new residents would be unable to support a bank.

Phyllis Betts (Otti) (1978) provides the best account of that endeavor and several other important organized community efforts to fight for desired consequences.

The movement to keep the bank in South Shore was organized by a white resident who had been born in the community and had lived his whole life there. Feeling that the symbolism of the move would administer the final death stroke to the community's fortunes, he organized a "Stop the Bank" committee. It never turned into a real social movement, but he was able to mobilize expert or near-expert testimony for an administrative hearing on the relocation request. His experts, mainly bank officials who lived in the area, plus a teacher of finance, testified that in order to survive, the community needed the bank and the capital it could provide. Also opposed to the move was a downtown bank, which was next to the proposed location for the South Shore bank. Its officers testified that such a move would be harmful to them and was also unnecessary.

A second hearing was called, and both sides were able to mobilize additional expert resources, the community turning to the Legal Aid Society for help. On December 5, 1972, the Comptroller of the Currency issued his decision. The bank was not permitted to shift its location. In what was an unusual move, he cited community needs as one of the components of his decision. It was shortly after this decision that Grzywinski and his group began negotiating for the bank.

It is important to note that this was not a mass community mobilization. It represented the efforts of a few concerned citizens who were able to mobilize some expert resources to make its case. It is also doubtful that they would have succeeded if the fear of competition had not brought a downtown bank in on their side.

"Stop the Bank" was not the last effort at community activism in South Shore, nor the only effective one. It does, however, illustrate the conditions and concerns of South Shore in August of 1973 as INDC management began work. It was a community on a downward slope. The crime rate was on the rise, as were welfare rates, tax delinquency rates on multiple-family dwellings, and vacancy rates along the main shopping strips. Its community organizations that had once been sources of great vitality were almost hollow shells. The bank itself faced a massive outflow of deposits, deferred maintenance, and a lack of concern with system development.

Let me now turn to the new management's first efforts to reverse those forces.

4

Strengthening the Bank

At bottom, development strategy involved getting more economic resources into the hands of South Shore residents. That meant making loans that were not currently being made elsewhere because of prejudice or a limited conception of what was possible. But there were other elements in the process as well. Just as the knowledge that the bank would stay in South Shore provided a certain measure of psychological uplift for the community, *how* the bank chose to position itself was also believed to have an important symbolic meaning. Therefore, almost all of the efforts in 1973 and 1974 of the bank to establish itself in the community were understood to have development consequences and so received an enormous amount of management attention. This was true of the decision to improve the physical plant as well.

The idea was that communities that were changing racially saw themselves being systematically abandoned by major societal institutions. Supermarket chains were closing branches, city services were declining in quality, and, indeed, the bank itself had almost left South Shore. Therefore, efforts to redo the bank's interior and exterior, to provide a state-of-the-art and attractive drive-in teller branch, as well as a new parking lot heavily landscaped with trees and plants, would send a positive message to the community: the bank was in

South Shore to stay, and the community was worthy of a heavy, first-class investment.

Implementation of some of these decisions, it should be added, was problematic. Indeed, it presaged further problems of doing development in the city. Aside from their high cost—these were expensive projects, in some cases designed by nationally known people (another example of the management belief in the symbolic importance of going first class)—there were other issues. For example, to build the parking lot close enough to the bank, two small six-flat buildings, in moderately deteriorated condition, had to go, forcing displacement. Even the fact that the lot had to be that close was in some sense a special problem for this type of neighborhood. Depositors, it was felt, would be afraid to walk very far. Employees who used the old lot had already complained about the distance (half a block and across the street), and at least two of them had been mugged in transit.

The decision to take down the two small buildings caused a slight chill nonetheless. Not only did management feel sensitive about the demolition—by then, displacing the poor for so-called development activities was anathema to those concerned about the poor—but also there were some ripples of discontent within the community.

The matter even came up at a meeting of the bank's board of directors. Its position was that if the bank failed, it ought to fail only after doing everything right. A decent parking lot was clearly a necessity. Second, at least one director felt that a successful bank would have such a positive impact on the community that it was worth the loss. Entrepreneurs would have no problem tearing down a few buildings, if wanting a successful bank were their only goal. Those who want to help the disadvantaged, however, are often paralyzed because they are afraid of doing more harm than good.

At any rate, after some soul-searching, bank management decided in 1976 to buy the buildings and tear them down. But all the guilt and ambivalence did not disappear. Bank employees told about the nice old man who sat at the window of one of those buildings and waved and smiled at people as they were heading for home at the end of the day. They had come to look forward to his warm and friendly smile. The day after the announcement was made that the buildings were to come down, he stopped smiling and waving. That hurt.

A sensitive development organization has to consider the costs of displacement that come with some forms of development. This is as it should be. But the question of displacement resurfaces whenever an INDC affiliate undertakes a project.

Another project that raised implementation problems was the drive-in teller. The old facility was inadequate and inefficient, a deterrent to prospective customers. A new location was selected, on the site of an abandoned supermarket building two blocks away on the edge of Jackson Park Highlands, which, with its big houses and broad lawns, was South Shore's fanciest and highest-status area. In keeping with the philosophy of going first class, bank officers selected an unobtrusive design, which included a small structure to house the tellers, who operated remote depository stands lined up neatly in a row. Like the parking lot, the area was landscaped heavily with trees to minimize the impact of a large expanse of asphalt. Bank management ran into two problems: the neighbors did not want it; some customers were afraid to use it.

In retrospect, the neighborhood reaction was predictable. One could see, however, why it caught bank officials by surprise. By replacing a crumbling retail building with a sparkling yet subtle new facility, they thought they were upgrading the area and that the facility's neighbors would be grateful. However, the substantial negative reaction consisted of two components.

The first was that residents did not want the additional traffic that such a facility would bring. This was not surprising. People often want new facilities for their community. But if those facilities threaten the disruption of their own situation, they want the facilities placed in another part of town. Any observer of zoning disputes is familiar with that. What was particularly surprising was the strength of the reaction. It was angry.

This response is worth special comment. The level of concern about the teller location exceeded, in fact, the fear neighbors had about too much traffic. That intensity was generated by general suspicion of INDC management and its motives. Suspicion of outsiders is often an important aspect of community life. One can find it easily in New England towns and in many of any city's ethnic neighborhoods. But that suspicion of outsiders, particularly of those who come bearing gifts or promising to do good, has a distinctive bite in the nation's minority communities. Outsiders normally come into those areas to do well for themselves rather than to do good for the community, but they often come with promises to do otherwise. To view such actors with suspicion is, then, not paranoia. For those who view themselves on the edge—that is, in a position where a little shove can knock them off—that suspicion takes on additional urgency.

In the early efforts to market the South Shore Bank, officials, particularly Grzywinski and Davis, spent long hours in "coffees," meeting with community members to report on their mission. The goal was both to allay fears and to generate deposits. Similarly, other marketing efforts emphasized that deposits in the bank would strengthen South Shore. Very little of this effort had the desired effect. Indeed, in at least one meeting, community residents whose welcome was often restrained said, "We've heard something like this before. Come back in a few years after we have seen what you have done."

Dealing with that suspicion and, in turn, generating trust were to become a continuing problem for INDC. In any community, this would be the case for outside agents who promised to become major actors. In this instance, the problem was compounded by the fact that management of INDC was disproportionately white and the community was mostly black.

It did not help that most of the top management came from Hyde Park, which was the home of the University of Chicago. Because the university had recently supervised a massive urban renewal project that helped to push some poor black people to South Shore, many black citizens viewed the university with distinct unease. There were more than a few residents of South Shore who saw the INDC as a kind of point man for the university, which would pursue policies in South Shore not dissimilar from those it had pursued in its home community. At any rate, we will see this set of issues resurface, sometimes out of real concern and sometimes used by those who wished to mobilize the community against some aspect of bank policy.

Seen in that light, the issue of traffic generation itself becomes quite small. The larger questions are first, about the intensity of community concern, and second, about the appropriate response. A sensitive response communicates understanding of the latent message and attempts to deal with that by sharing information, which management did in this instance. At the same time, management did not allow itself to be paralyzed by the community complaint, and, having made its case, went ahead with the project.

When the drive-in teller facility opened in early 1976, it did not generate the volume of new business that bank officials had hoped. One reason illustrates another problem of doing business in the city. When it was not very busy, customers were afraid to use the facility. Ironically, the efforts to make the facility attractive and unobtrusive made it instead a frightening place to be. It seemed to potential customers that they would be pulling their cars into a broad empty expanse that had the additional liability of all that shrubbery, which could hide potential robbers while shielding from view the passing public. This configuration made them sitting ducks. The teller facility became more successful, however, when a guard was posted, ostensibly to answer questions and help direct traffic.

MARKETING THE BANK

Just as making the bank attractive was seen as both a marketing and a development effort, initially, generating deposits had a dual function. The bank had to move its level of deposits beyond $38 million if it were to have the resources available to lend and thereby encourage development. But in addition, there was the view, widely held in the organization, that bank deposits generated income for the small saver.

In those early days (1973 and 1974), there was much talk about how currency exchanges charged excessive money for the services they provided, and about how the poor were burdened excessively because they were required to pay for services that the middle class received for nothing. Some members of the fresh management team actually calculated the savings accruing to individual community members who switched from currency exchanges to the bank. The totals ran from five to ten dollars a month.

Similarly, bank managers had an almost mythical conception of savings accounts. The theory was that if the bank reduced all minimum balances to a dollar, reduced service charges, and simplified procedures to open new accounts, many low-income people would be encouraged to open savings accounts, which they would have the opportunity to watch grow.

In 1987, since the consequences of bank deregulation have become apparent and sophisticated cost accounting has demonstrated that retail banking, particularly that aimed at those with small balances, is an expensive activity for any bank, this idea seems foolishly romantic. But one has to be careful, when observing these matters, not to impose on the past the contemporary insights that changing economic conditions have now made abundantly clear.

In that spirit, management evaluated the procedures for opening new accounts. They turned out to be unbelievably cumbersome and a barrier for the new and sometimes unsophisticated customers the bank wanted. So an effort was made to simplify and speed the procedures.

The combination of increasing hours, simplifying procedures, reducing minimum balance requirements, and providing parking and drive-up teller facilities should have increased bank deposits. The bank did attract new depositors by lowering the barriers, but the total amount of money in deposits did not discernibly rise. This lack was understood as partly a consequence of the continued withdrawal of funds by old depositors who had moved away or had lost confidence in the neighborhood. Bank officials were confident that that trend would run its course and that the new residents in the community had substantial resources, which would find their way into the bank as the neighbors discovered that the bank was friendly to them and was also investing in the area. The bankers knew the deposits were out there. In determining whether South Shore residents could continue to support the bank, they discovered that downtown banks held more than $90 million of deposits from people in the South Shore. This figure did not even include funds deposited with savings and loan associations.

Numerous people opened new accounts. It seemed as if the new friendliness were working. The bank lobby was an absolute madhouse on Saturday mornings as mobs of people wandered through and others stood waiting in what became interminably long teller lines. In a sense, the crowds presented an agreeable hubbub. Old friends called to each other across the lobby. People came to do business in clusters and chatted amiably. The bank even provided coffee and doughnut holes for customers.

But beneath that cheerful hubbub was another sound, and that was the grinding of teeth in frustration. The teller lines were too long. The former owners had not invested much in efficiency, so that even in 1974, the bank had no on-line computer systems to deal with the business. Tellers had to consult ledgers to check balances—especially for those with savings accounts—and most other procedures were comparable in speed and efficiency. Increasingly, people were visiting bank officials to complain. The person visited most often was the president, Milton Davis, who, with an office on the first floor, was informally responsible for public relations, complaints, and troubleshooting. He, too, was increasingly agitated. He would step out into the lobby to see that all teller windows were manned, and duck back into the office, exasperated at the delays and confusion.

Teller managers were rotated. New systems slowly were put into place. But the total picture, even by late 1974, was not positive. First, most of the new accounts were small. In addition, unaccustomed to savings accounts, many new depositors used their savings accounts like checking accounts.

Large numbers of small accounts were being churned—to borrow a term from another part of the financial world. South
Shore's depositors kept small and busy accounts, which they
had to visit frequently. The problem was compounded by some
of the old customers, elderly whites who had not left the
community. They often had several small accounts, and it
was a big outing for them to go to the bank and bring their
accounts up to date. In order to avoid extra-long delays, experienced customers developed expertise in spotting little old
ladies with three or four passbooks. A third component of the
delays arose from managerial fear of fraud and theft. Some
bank officials felt that the bank's declaration that it was committed to the community as a whole seemed to mean that the
bank was a soft touch, easy to cheat. The bank was hit by
waves of people opening accounts with dubious checks and
trying to get back cash from their initial deposits, people who
opened large accounts with fraudulent checks and then tried
to cash their own, and individuals trying to cash stolen welfare
and other government checks. During the transition period,
some of the older bank employees became very zealous about
identifying thieves. Onerous systems that were slow, cumbersome, and slightly insulting to customers were instituted. No
downtown bank, for example, required two pieces of personal
identification to cash one's own personal check or asked what
someone's mother's maiden name was.

   The long delays, coupled with the attitude those delays com-
municated to customers, were just the sort to irritate those
new depositors who were the kind of people the bank was
trying to attract—that is, who had substantial resources and
would be likely to maintain large balances. Some of them tried
the bank by opening small second accounts. It took only one
Saturday morning at the bank for many of them to decide that
they did not want to spend any more time there ever. They
did not have lines and waits like this at their downtown banks,
nor did they have to experience what they interpreted as racial
insults—which is how they interpreted such questions as
"What was your mother's maiden name?" and in their own
community, no less.

In a general way, nobody was really at fault. There were numerous attempts at fraud. For example, bank officials proudly told the story of refusing to give money back to a new depositor out of a $10,000 cashier's check drawn on the biggest bank in the city. They called the originating bank and were told that cashier's checks were as good as cash. Nonetheless, there was something about the transaction that made the bank's cashier uneasy, and he refused to pay out the money right away, insisting that he would hold the check for a few days. It was subsequently discovered by the issuing bank that the check had been stolen, and that the South Shore Bank had been correct in not paying on it. The cashier became a hero, and visitors heard the story from several individuals, all of whom were pleased. But imagine the response to that kind of delay by the ordinary black middle-class customer who finds his bank refusing to credit a cashier's check written by the biggest bank in the city. Would similar customers under similar circumstances be hassled if they were white? Some South Shore residents said as much.

In addition, the system in general was not ready for the deluge. I have described the system of checking balances on ledgers. There were other operational systems that were similarly antiquated, slow, and/or cumbersome. And, inevitably, mistakes were made. There is some dispute about whether the South Shore Bank made more mistakes than downtown banks, but reports of errors were legion. Furthermore, as management acknowledged, South Shore probably had to do better than downtown banks if it were to persuade people to move their accounts to it. At any rate, given the other difficulties, often new depositors who had other choices did not continue to bank at South Shore for long.

Even though systems improved, the bigger deposits did not come rolling in. Officials developed a protective ideology. Black people, they said, like the prestige of brand names. They like the idea of having their accounts at a prestigious downtown bank. Some even added with a sneer that people preferred to bank on their employer's time (downtown) than they did on their own (in the community). Bank officials thought enough of the idea to develop a hard-hitting multimedia presentation (slide show with background voice and music), which emphasized this perspective. "All you get downtown is prestige," the voice said. "In South Shore, you get personal service and investment in your neighborhood." But aside from offering potential customers the opportunity to invest in their own community, the bank could offer few counterattractions (no pun). Personal service, after all, is no substitute for good service.

In those early days, the bank marketed itself in other ways. It launched a campaign involving loaves of bread to encourage people to bring their "bread" to the bank. (The bimonthly publication the *Bread Rapper* is a current descendant of that effort, focusing on community business and events and on bank development efforts.) There was a plan in which church and community groups would get certain bonuses if they brought accounts to the bank—a plan so complicated that most potential customers could not understand it. Although it resisted the idea of giving premiums because they were not sufficiently classy, the bank even tried giving away everything from charcoal grills to house plants. None of the campaigns increased total deposits. The lobby, however, was busier than ever. The bank employee responsible for marketing reported that his efforts had been the biggest collective failure of his entire life.

In short, new deposits were not being generated in a way that led to total deposit growth, and the bank's profit position in those first years was not such that there was much money to spend on development.

THE BANK AND THE COMMUNITY

Bank management came into contact with the community through its crowded lobbies, interviews with numerous potential customers, and various marketing efforts. Grzywinski and Davis attended a series of evening "coffees" to meet important people in the community and learned about the level of dissatisfaction people felt for the old bank management. They also learned that many black middle-class people disapproved of the poor. They found themselves in the middle of arguments about the stance one should take toward the poor (drive them out or help them) and toward those members of the black subculture who dressed in flashy clothes and drove flashy cars. But the level of attendance at these events was never very large, and it became clear that as community input went, this was a limited source.

This was the mid-1970s, just after the zenith of community-power concerns in the United States and, as I discussed in chapter 2, management had a commitment to building formal ties to the community. The early planning for the bank even included community shares and ultimately community ownership. That part of the program was never implemented.

The fact that the bank did not work closely with the community in a formal sense requires additional explanation. Much of the literature on community economic development emphasizes the importance of community participation in decision making and development activity. For a community to have economic development, the argument goes, its members must be mobilized and brought into the process. As they help shape outcomes, their sense of efficacy will increase and they will become more wholehearted participants. Similarly, through their participation, their interests will be protected, and they will feel less threatened by the constructive change taking place around them. Finally, it is argued, by having community members involved, those doing the planning will be sensitive to nuance and will be able to judge accurately both key actors in the community and the ramifications of any course of action.

The intellectual tradition pursuing this orientation has sturdy roots, going back at least to Alexis de Tocqueville (Taub and Taub, 1974). It is a view that finds resonance throughout American society with its antielitist and populist traditions.

This viewpoint is so widely held and accepted that if the South Shore Bank had built community ties of the participatory type, I would be able to report it without detailed justification. To borrow from Thomas Kuhn (1962), one could say that that approach is a paradigmatic conception of the way things are.

But the Illinois Neighborhood Development Corporation has not done that. What is striking about INDC is that it has kept the community at a distance. Its efforts to generate formal relations with community groups have been ambivalent. And, as some of its critics have argued, it has not been the source of a ground swell of community involvement in local organizational behavior. In the second year of operation, and after some soul-searching, the bank created a citizens' advisory board. Management settled on a carefully selected group of property owners representing some of the subareas within the community and having a reputation for community leadership. Although the board lasted four years, and for much of that period met once a month, and also participated in some stimulating "retreats," its relationship to the bank never was well delineated. Board members and bank managers were uneasy with each other, and the two groups never agreed on how they could be useful to each other. The board wanted to help the bank make policy vis-à-vis the community, but nobody really understood what that involved. It also saw itself as providing a kind of quality control, checking out service and treatment of customers. In those days, service was so bad that there was a great deal to say on the subject, but board criticism often seemed carping and trivial to management. For example, a bank guard was reprimanded for calling a black man "boy." Bank management wanted to use the board as a marketing tool and a sounding board for new products. The board did not know how it felt about doing that. And so, uneasily, but more or less side by side, the bank and its citizen advisors marched into the future.

One good symbol of the problem was an issue that surfaced at the first meeting. During the renovation of the building the bank had removed a large clock that adorned the facade. Almost the first request of the citizens' board was to reinstall the clock. Residents had complained that they used the clock to judge how prompt they were on their way to work, and that they now missed its presence.

From management's point of view, this looked like an absolutely trivial matter. Having just spent a large sum of money on upgrading the appearance of the bank, they were slightly annoyed that their efforts were being inadequately appreciated. They had priced out a new clock, and it seemed inordinately expensive. That first meeting symbolized what was to come. The group met less and less frequently, until finally its activities melted away.

The bank also tried developing closer ties to the South Shore Commission. Milton Davis even served as president of the commission for one term in 1976. The year before, at INDC's urging, the Joyce Foundation had given an $80,000 grant to the commission so that it could purchase stock in INDC. The relationship between the commission and the bank never strengthened. There was also an effort made to have at least one community resident qua resident on INDC's board as a kind of community agent. Over time, members of the community who served on the bank's and holding company's boards were chosen, not especially to be community representatives but because they brought special expertise and talents to the group.

INDC was never completely cut off from the community. Davis was a South Shore resident. His wife was active in one of the local churches. Bank management knew many residents as customers. But efforts to relate systematically to the community did, in fact, dwindle away.

Relating more closely to the community, particularly its lower-income component, was later to become the responsibility of The Neighborhood Institute, an affiliate created partly for that purpose. As we shall see, that is another task it achieved less well than had been hoped.

In conclusion, serious, committed, and continuous community involvement was never a large part of the bank program nor was it ever achieved. At times, INDC personnel have made fruitful contact with individual community residents. At other times, INDC and some community groups have worked together on a specific issue. At least as often, they have disagreed. For those who see involved and substantial community participation in the decision-making process as an important component of neighborhood redevelopment, the South Shore model would be a disappointment.

As I shall try to show, however, an arm's-length approach to the community has benefits when seen from a development perspective. What is often the case is that community action is in opposition to development efforts. The possibility of development activity unleashes a great deal of self-interested behavior. Residents ask, "What is in it for us? What will this do to us?" For many people who perceive themselves on the edge of a precipice overlooking dramatic neighborhood decline, any change seems threatening to most and possibly rewarding only to a lucky few, who may, as far as anybody knows, be preying on the community. In such a situation, a group with the capacity to act, to make decisions, and ultimately to provide positive symbols to rally round, may be more important than the backing and filling which community involvement so often generates.

An assertion of this sort is open to the criticism that authoritarian behavior always seems more efficient than democratic behavior, but its ultimate costs may be very high. (For example, Mussolini made the trains run on time.) Ford Foundation officials have asserted for many years that their successful inner-city development activities have been led by strong-willed authoritarian types who will not put up with nonsense. This approach is not exactly analogous to what I am talking about, but it makes a similar point. The question in this context is what other forces make the agency accountable: that is, to see that it does not trample on local concerns and that it lives up to its mandate. In the case of the INDC, it is primarily the shareholders of the corporation and the members of its board who must judge the nature and type of INDC achievements. On narrow investment decisions, it has to reckon only with the conscience of management and the oversight of its board. On communitywide issues, it has often disagreed with groups in the community and has sometimes won and sometimes lost. On matters where city approval is required for federal subsidy, it has had to deal directly with concerned community groups and individuals (many of whom call themselves groups in order to provide legitimacy). In this sense, the requirements set by law accomplished what they were intended to. As we look at INDC's substantial achievements, we will see that it has been dramatically effective, and in ways that are not destructive of community values.

So far, I have focused on matters related to the start-up of INDC activities in South Shore. And, in some ways, I have presented a picture that is not promising—lots of early enthusiasm, some mistakes, some blurring of focus, ambivalence toward community involvement, and the like. Yet, the INDC as it has developed has been a dramatic success.

What I propose to do in the next few chapters is to focus on the bank's early lending activities, and follow that discussion with some other initiatives of INDC that were to have clear consequences. These include attracting involvement and investments from outside the community, the development of the Parkside Banker program, and, ultimately, the organization of other subsidiaries of INDC, City Lands, and The Neighborhood Institute.

Then, I shall sort through what we have learned in order to understand how best to pursue the difficult goal of urban economic development and how the community and INDC reached the position they are in today.

5

Early Lending Activities

In addition to fixing up the bank and working on building relations with the community, bank officials were involved in hammering out lending programs. "Disinvestment," the withdrawal of economic support for the purchase and maintenance of buildings and businesses, is often considered the cause of neighborhood decline, and it is in the area of providing investment resources that INDC management saw its mission. It was, as well, the area in which the new management had had the most successful experience before coming to South Shore.

It was as lenders in the urban development division of the Hyde Park Bank that Grzywinski, Houghton, Davis, and Fletcher had first come together. There they had built a substantial national reputation in the late 1960s, lending funds in productive and successful ways to black entrepreneurs when other banks were reluctant to make such loans. As the four are proud of pointing out, they had helped provide the resources that ultimately produced several black millionaires. With that historical experience in mind, let me turn, then, to lending activities in South Shore.

Generally speaking, banks make three different types of loans: consumer, commercial, and real estate. South Shore Bank, in theory, was making all three when the new management took over in 1973. At that time, however, the old management had been making hardly any loans. This was partly because of the uncertainty generated by the racial change in the neighborhood, and partly because of a need to maintain a strong cash position, which would help facilitate the bank's sale.

Consumer loans, small loans taken out in order to purchase items that then serve as collateral, were moving at a low level. If there are not too many defaults, this type of loan is usually profitable, because a bank charges high interest rates on it. The South Shore Bank, however, had inherited a great deal of bad paper resulting from one of the recurrent scandals of the FHA in the inner city. In this instance, it was a federally supported home-improvement program. Typically, the improvements were not made or were made badly, and, sometimes with the collusion of the home owner and sometimes without, the home repair company pocketed a tidy profit. This kind of loan was often uncollectible, and the bank found itself with too many of them.

Following what was then customary banking practice, the first commercial loan officer the new management inherited was not predisposed to make loans to blacks unless their economic situation was absolutely blue chip. Although no evidence could be found that he was actually prejudiced in making his credit judgments, he was encouraged to broaden his loan portfolio. Unfortunately, it is difficult to teach a person to change his standards of judgment. If people are cut loose from their anchors, they are likely to drift farther than one might hope. Many of the loans made during that early period were defaulted on, and the bank had some difficulty finding someone who could manage the commercial loan operation successfully. Such an officer had to be tough but not rude, kind but not soft, and accustomed to dealing with customers some of whose personal styles were not commonly seen in banks, either downtown or in ethnic neighborhoods.

The bank's official attitude toward consumer loans was to vary a great deal in the succeeding ten years. Sometimes it saw them as an adjunct to development activity (increasing the purchasing power of the black community), other times as a dangerous enticement to get people into levels of consumer debt from which they might not recover. At still others, the loans were viewed as a service the bank should provide and one that would make life easier for local residents. When the bank's earnings were particularly disappointing, consumer loans, especially for automobiles, were seen as a profit opportunity; but it became clear, over time, that consumer lending as a major source of revenue was a chimera. People did not break down the doors to get the loans, collection costs were high, and there were default problems.

The old bank management had not, in the early 1970s, been vigorously involved in new commercial lending, either, and the only loans made in South Shore were to the old customers of long-term good standing. The old-line personnel treated these loan customers with exceptional courtesy. They never had to wait in lines, and bank officers serviced the deposits themselves. The bank had participated with other banks in extending lines of credit to big national corporations, but lending to local black customers was not high on their list of priorities.

In contrast, new management placed commercial lending at the head of their development program and aggressively set out to make loans. One of the first was to a man named Conrad Brown. He owned a complex of stores, including a sort of supermarket-department store and a laundromat near the bank. He needed $15,000 to fix up his complex, and he hoped the bank would lend him the money. If management was serious about helping black people, he told them, his loan would be a real opportunity to demonstrate the fact.

Davis and Grzywinski, who were clearly experts on lending to black entrepreneurs, were delighted. They were amazed that the previous owners had never made a loan to Brown, evidence to them of the racist policies of the old management. Brown was an example of the classic, aggressive West Indian entrepreneur everybody knew about. He had started with the department store, and was expanding into the stores adjacent to it. He carried everything from liquor and food to handbags and pen-and-pencil sets. Like the stores of ambitious small merchants everywhere, his shop was open long hours, as well as Sundays and holidays. South Shore residents knew that if they needed almost anything at odd times, they could find it at Conrad's.

He was full of ideas for expansion. He had his eye on vacant property behind the store. He was driving a nearby laundromat out of business by opening his own next door to it. In short, he looked like the perfect loan customer—aggressive, go-getting, hard working, and smart. From the bank's point of view, this request was a good augury. Directly across from the bank, on the main intersection of the busiest shopping strip, there were also a Walgreens drugstore and a Woolworth. A successful shop would strengthen that important location and Brown was only the beginning. There seemed to be other businessmen along that strip who looked promising. They included a tavern owner and a bicycle shop owner, both of whom seemed to know what they were doing.

The bank loaned Conrad his $15,000. Time passed, and then his name started coming up at loan committee meetings. He was behind on his payments, but he worked out a new method of paying back the loan. He was not answering letters or telephone calls. He met with bank lawyers to work out another repayment schedule. Indeed, after several years, he did clear up most of that first loan.

The story had an even more distressing sequel. Early in 1977, upset beyond the powers of self-control, Brown struck and tied up two Small Business Administration officials who had come to foreclose on his store, because he had defaulted on another loan to another bank, and to estimate what could be recovered by liquidation. He poured kerosene over them and ignited them, along with his store. They died, and the store burned to the ground.

Today the Walgreens occupies a new store built on the old Conrad's location. It appears to be prosperous and busy, but it casts its own sort of blight on the shopping strip. With gray brick walls right to the sidewalk, no windows, and a heavy iron gate, it broadcasts to the world that "this corner is a dangerous place."

Although it is the most dramatic one, the Conrad's story is not the only one to end tragically. The owner of a successful liquor store (and a member of the bank's community advisory board) put to his head a gun he said was empty, and fired it. A few months before that, he had reported to friends when he sympathized with Conrad. There were times, he said, that he felt so thin and stretched out, facing more personal demands than he could manage, that he thought the only way was suicide. Entrepreneurs in most places face difficult struggles. It may be that operating a successful business in a neighborhood that appears to be declining, and doing so with no family tradition of entrepreneurship to teach one how to take the shocks and balance diverse interests, generate a special set of pressures.

THE DEVELOPMENT DIVISION

To handle difficult commercial loans, the bank created a development division. Headed by Mary Houghton, this was *the* hot place to be in the bank. It was where the "knowers" focused their energy. Also tied to the growth of the development division was one of the bank's major innovations, beginning in 1974: the development deposit. People residing outside South Shore who had records of contributing to liberal causes were solicited for deposits through a direct-mail campaign. The argument alluded to earlier—that is, that the bank provided the same services depositors could get from their own bank, but deposit dollars in the South Shore Bank would "do good"—became the main theme for the campaign. By mid-1976, there was a development audit that reported to depositors on the impact of the income from their deposits. Development deposits not only paid for the extra costs of making development loans, they became major contributors to the survival and profitability of the bank. Local deposits never rose to the levels management had hoped for. One of the old members of management who stayed on for a few years was quite certain that development deposits were the "new wrinkle" that made "this type of bank"—that is, a bank in a black neighborhood with a development focus—possible.

A sage might want to dwell on the fact that outside the community, direct mail with the theme of helping South Shore was more successful in attracting deposits than promotions with similar themes ever were within the community. It should be pointed out, however, that the potential population of depositors nationwide is much larger than that within South Shore. And the proportion of people with discretionary dollars is larger still.

Other early commercial loans went bad, even though bank officials devoted long hours to working with the recipients. One of them was a loan to help start a building management firm. The logic that went into creating the firm was impeccable. White management firms seemed to have a difficult time managing buildings in the ghetto. Because many of them had the same prejudices I have discussed earlier, they often assumed, prematurely, that buildings could not make a profit, and that, consequently, the buildings should be milked. In addition, like some of the bank's consumer loan officers, many white management firms did not know how to deal with the new residents. Finally, the bank concluded that a locally owned and operated company might keep more money within the community and provide more local employment opportunities than one owned and operated by whites.

The trick was to identify an experienced black manager with building management experience and encourage him to start his own business. Such a man was found, and his company was funded through a Small Business Administration guaranteed loan. It was not long before he had a substantial number of buildings to manage.

Although bank staff people spent an enormous amount of time working with him, that project failed. Whatever the reason, it became clear that some of the buildings he was supposed to manage were not being handled very well, and soon he became delinquent on his payments, ultimately defaulting.

The bank staff had developed substantial expertise in packaging SBA loans. But the early ones were not conspicuously successful. For example, a loan of more than $100,000 to a laundromat owner did not work out very well, despite hundreds of hours of assistance from bank personnel. In short, the considerable expertise in commercial lending to minorities that bank personnel brought to South Shore did not seem to pay off. The costs of making commercial loans were very high in terms of time, even with SBA loans as a component. Although there have been conspicuous achievements as well as failures, it is safe to say that the commercial loan program at South Shore has never been a success. It has produced or supported few South Shore entrepreneurs. It has not so far generated the business activity on Seventy-first Street, the community's main shopping street, that was hoped for, and it has absorbed a great deal of staff time. I will discuss Seventy-first Street in more detail in chapter 7 and, at the same time, consider the reasons why commercial lending has not been as successful as had been hoped.

REAL ESTATE LENDING

It was in the area of real estate lending, particularly that for single-family houses, that one could see the most dramatic and historic effects of racial discrimination. Many residents could not get mortgages at all or could get only those guaranteed by the FHA and provided by mortgage companies, some of which seemed to make their money by "fast foreclosure." There are obvious costs of not being able to get mortgages. One is that when houses cannot be sold through the mortgage structure, they must be rented out or sold on contract, both of which methods generate obvious problems for house owners who may have their life savings tied up in the property. Another is that the costs to a community of operating only in the FHA credit world are very high. Because such mortgages were guaranteed, those making the loans did not do enough careful credit screening. This meant that a fairly large proportion of home buyers were not really appropriate candidates to buy a house. The mortgage companies got paid not only for making the loans but also for foreclosing on them, and units that entered the cycle of purchase and foreclosure did nothing for their immediate surroundings. Foreclosed buildings were required by law to be boarded up for a year (undergoing substantial deterioration, generated by the elements and by vandals) before any final disposition of the structure was permitted. The boarded-up structures cast a blight on the buildings around them, communicating to potential purchasers that the neighborhood clearly was on its way down. Consequently, for a community to break into the conventional mortgage world was to give it a new opportunity for survival.

It was in this area that South Shore Bank lending first made its mark. The man in charge of real estate loans had been a member of the old South Shore Bank management team. He had been responsible for real estate lending for some time, but he had not been allowed to lend money on real estate except to a few of the bank's special customers. In 1972, only two mortgages were made, totaling $59,000.

To hear him tell it, he sat under a sign that said, "Real Estate Loans." But his job was to specify such conditions as a 40 percent down payment, high charges for "points," and other onerous components which would discourage purchasers. In his view, this practice had not been motivated by racial prejudice as much as by bank management's not wanting to have a lot of paper out while it was trying to sell the institution. Now he had the opportunity to make real mortgages and to put to work the expertise he had gained over many years.

The first loans could be classified as "cream skimming." They were the absolutely and unambiguously good mortgages by any standard. They went to two-earner families whose combined annual incomes were close to the purchase price of the house (a rule of thumb for making mortgages is that the purchase price not exceed twice the annual family income), and who had had long and stable careers. The houses for which they were seeking mortgages tended to be located on the best blocks and in the best areas. It may not have seemed like much of a breakthrough, but in the face of actual redlining and the failure of other banks to grant mortgages in the area, it was an important first step.

As management saw these mortgages going only to the best houses, an effort was made to expand mortgage activity further, encouraging realtors to bring mortgage candidates to the bank and spreading the word that mortgages on conventional terms were available. Many residents with less than perfect records were reluctant to walk into a bank to be turned down. Part of the bank's marketing challenge was how to move into a more aggressive and development-oriented posture. It was clear that South Shore was skidding, and waiting for walk-in business was not the way to reverse matters.

To protect the bank while it was lending aggressively, management also made use of private mortgage insurance. Although this practice does generate extra paperwork, it reduces the risk and inspires confidence, as SBA loan guarantees do. One important achievement of bank management was to persuade the Milwaukee Guarantee Insurance Company (MGIC) to provide that insurance for a minority neighborhood.

It was also true that providing single-family home mortgages was not in itself a way to turn South Shore around, for single-family homes accounted for only about 15 percent of all the housing units within the community. This was a hard fact for both the bank and community residents to come to grips with. It may sound so obvious that it is hardly worth saying, but single-family housing is low density: that is, a small number of units take up lots of space. The majority of the territory in South Shore is covered by single-family houses, and residents and some observers tend to think of the area as a community of houses. Large housing units hold as many as 300 families. In detached single-family home terms in South Shore, that means an area five blocks wide by four blocks deep, so the area is mainly one of apartments. It is important to make this point, because any attack on South Shore's problems would have to target multiple-family dwellings.

Many of these buildings constituted the soft underbelly of the community. Attractive in strong stable neighborhoods, they became liabilities in declining or threatened neighborhoods. Indeed, in people's minds the transformation of courtyard architecture from a positive attribute to a negative one because of changes in the community is a classic example of the process whereby physical attributes defined as desirable by community residents and investors in stable neighborhoods take on a negative character in those areas undergoing destabilization. In a secure neighborhood, the open courtyards provide open space and fresh air. The separate entryways help build friendliness among the residents who share them. The apartments tend to be large and airy. When South Shore was unambiguously middle-class and white, the buildings constituted an attraction. (Even in a stable Chicago community, these U-shaped buildings have some liabilities. The absence of elevators and the economic impossibility of installing them for each entry reduce their attractiveness to older people who must negotiate the stairs. But that is another story.)

In a declining community, that picture changes. The buildings are old and require substantial maintenance and renovation. Because of the decline, landlords do not believe they can charge the rents necessary to cover the costs of upkeep. In addition, the very aspects of these buildings that are attractive in the stable world are now problems. The open courtyard and the separate entryways are places for muggers to hide, ready to pounce on unwary victims. During the day after school and on weekends, the courtyards often reverberate with the shouts of unsupervised children at play, creating a disturbance for those who prefer peace and quiet. The separate doorways also make it more difficult to control access by potential criminals. Finally, the spacious units are easily broken up into smaller units either by the tenants or by the landlords, in which case crowding and transiency bring with them a host of new undesirable attributes.

In a 1978 study by the city of Chicago, it was determined that such buildings were the ones most likely to be abandoned first in a neighborhood and most likely to be tax-delinquent. South Shore was full of such structures: old multiple-family, walk-up apartment buildings owned by absentee landlords who were more interested in the size of the monthly check from obliging management companies than they were in the future of their properties. I do not suggest that there were large numbers of South Shore building owners who fit the allegedly classic slumlord mold. Lower incomes and, consequently, lower rents from new residents, added to an inability to get financing, meant that owners saw buildings with no future value and wanted to get their cash out quickly.

To tackle this problem required strategies beyond the single-family home mortgage—although, as we shall see, there were numerous smaller buildings, particularly of two to six flats, where a similar strategy with a few refinements would pay off. The larger multiple-family-dwelling problem, however, called for a solution beyond the reach of the small investor. It called for bringing outside investors into the community and helping them find subsidized funds. I shall turn in chapter 6 to the strategies devised for dealing with multiple-family buildings.

In sum, it is fair to say that in those early years the South Shore Bank made some false starts in the lending area but began to lay the groundwork for a solid future. The use of consumer and commercial lending did not get off to a promising start. In contrast, the mortgage seemed to provide a promising tool for upgrading the community, and that and the attraction of subsidized outside investors became the way for the bank to enter decisively into the South Shore economy.

6

Taking Initiatives

With all of the initial pieces in place, the bank management realized that much more had to be done before the bank could begin to move toward its goals. To do so, the managers went outside the bank for new expertise and outside the community for a fresh infusion of resources.

THE ARRIVAL OF TOM HEAGY

By late 1974, it was clear that management needed help. The old managers were unable to make the bank really profitable, and bank examiners were expressing some alarm about profits, loan quality, and the crucial ratios, such as capital-to-assets, that they used both to measure a bank's health and to ensure ongoing stability.

As I mentioned earlier, the bank's new managers were primarily interested in economic development, and they were not the sort of people who had the skills or, perhaps, interest to manage the bank's day-to-day operations.

They had offered high-ranking managerial positions to individuals who might admirably fill the role, but, although some people initially expressed interest, none followed through. Basically, the kinds of people who received offers were already working in relatively large, well-known, and prestigious

organizations. The opportunity to work in a small neighborhood bank seemed less than enticing. A move to South Shore
meant a decline in status; besides, the long-term prospects of
the bank were not of the same order as those of the organizations for which they worked.

Management hoped that black managers might be attracted
to the bank by its mission. That strategy, however, was about
as successful at attracting managers as the promise of South
Shore development activity was at attracting local depositors.
Ambitious black managers did not see South Shore as the
route to go. In many people's eyes, the whole bank effort was
an untried experiment with a potentially doubtful outcome.
It is important in this regard to remember that the leadership
of INDC was not composed of orthodox figures from the corporate world, either. To somebody who was operating in the
big time, the credentials of his prospective new employers and
colleagues could not have seemed very impressive.

University of Chicago Business School faculty members re-
garded our study as an unparalleled opportunity to track an
organization as it failed. They thought the bank could not last.
Even those who thought it could survive did not have much
hope for its impact on the community. An executive of a
federal funding agency from a banking family announced flatly
to a group of students and faculty members that there was no
way in which such an organization could have an impact on
the area.

Management, however, was finally able to recruit twenty-
nine-year-old Tom Heagy for the position in June 1975. Heagy
had been a University of Chicago undergraduate, and he held
master's degrees from the University of Chicago Business
School and the London School of Economics. A doctoral can-
didate at the Chicago Business School, he had worked at
Chicago's First National Bank full-time for five years, and
subsequent to that, he had served the bank as a consultant.
An expert in finance, he had spent most of his time at First
National staffing analytic positions.

He saw the South Shore Bank as a special high-risk, high-gain
opportunity. If he could become chairman of the board and

chief operating officer of the bank while still under thirty, he would be holding a position of unusual responsibility for one so young. In career terms, this would compensate for the fact that the bank was so small. In addition, if he turned the earnings of the bank around, he would not only gain financially (he arranged to have his salary pegged to profits), but he would have a dramatic accomplishment to show the world.

Heagy was as close to being somebody with an orthodox business and banking background as anyone the new management had yet hired. He knew he was there to straighten things out. As he put it, "Intellectually and even morally I have some interest in development. But that is not why I am here."

He came to the bank with a strong commitment to reduce staff size—with 110 employees, the bank was very large for an organization with only about $40 million in deposits; to cut deadwood; to improve service dramatically, partly through the development of new systems and partly through greater efficiency; and to institute a series of service charges and other fees that would cover the costs of low-balance deposits and the high rates of activity of such accounts.

The old management had begun to move gingerly in the direction of service charges from its initial position of being open and free to all as a means of encouraging banking activity. It had become obvious that this was economically impossible. The move to service charges generated a great deal of anxiety among its proponents because it represented a big departure and because it would discourage low-balance accounts—that is, the accounts of the relatively poor.

Heagy had few qualms.

... New charges on savings accounts ... will have the effect of closing out a lot of the very small accounts ... instead of giving a dollar's worth of free service each to ten thousand people, every month, say, which is a hundred thousand dollars a year; I would rather use that for some very specific program such as building redevelopment.

That is the strategy I have tried to follow ... you can get anything you want as long as you pay for it. We still have a long way to go in the savings area, I think.

Most of his effort in the bank, particularly during 1975 and 1976, however, was not devoted to identifying inefficiencies, but rather to active involvement in the bond market.

He joined the bank during a bull market in the bond world. With his background in bond pricing and his high level of financial acumen, he was able to enter the market with gusto and to turn a substantial profit. That profit was not from operations, as it should be to demonstrate basic bank strength, but through activity in the market. Since many people in the bank were frustrated with efforts to straighten out the bank's operations and make it profitable, there was even some talk about how they might live with unprofitable operations— maybe they were necessary in the sort of community South Shore was—and make their profits in the bond market. Wouldn't it be ironic, people said, to finance development activities through the bond market?

The bond market, however, would not be bullish forever; indeed, it soon ceased to be a major source of income. Fee income from condominium conversions in some of South Shore's largest buildings seemed to have similar potential. The bank was paid a fee by the developer for agreeing to provide mortgages to all qualified candidates, and a fee for each mortgage was provided. For a building with 300 units, the income could add up. This program caused controversy in the bank. The required level of down payment for some of the deals seemed low (10 percent on a $30,000 purchase in some instances), making it possible for people with small savings to purchase units on the one hand, but also making it easy for them to walk away from them if things did not go well.

The big income from that market, however, did not materialize. There was competition from other banks. Many of the condominium deals did not attract customers at all. In fact, several efforts at major conversions completely failed. Even Grzywinski's own brother did not succeed in his second effort.

By the end of his tenure, Heagy was feeling some frustration. With the decline of the bond market, external sources of income were indeed scarce. The bank tried to make money through consumer loans, particularly car loans, but hoped-for profits did not materialize there, either. The bank continued to put a great deal of effort into attracting new depositors through a series of promotions, but the new local depositors failed to arrive. Most of the only deposit growth came from development deposit solicitations.

By April of 1978, Heagy had almost given up. He saw no way to increase the profits of operations. "I have no more rabbits to pull out of hats," he said, "and I do not know what to do next."

In some sense, he underrated his achievement. He had introduced new products, which were to serve as the basis for future deposit growth. These included the elsewhere hot certificates of deposit, and Prestige Accounts, which provided a bundle of services for those with deposits over $1,000, and spared them the long and dreary teller lines. Like the initial effort to introduce service charges, which drove small depositors out of the bank, the idea of Prestige Accounts went against much management grain. It seemed undemocratic and inconsistent with the image and aspirations of a neighborhood bank. Such an approach, however, did have tremendous appeal to many neighborhood residents. Having made it into the middle class, they wanted special treatment and the symbols that went with it. They wanted to be treated as the comfortable, secure people they in fact were.

Initially, however, the new products did not have great appeal, mainly because the bank was not able to deliver the quality of service it promised. It made mistakes; too many people were curt or rude; and different systems were not properly integrated. A customer with $50,000 in CDs, for example, might be service-charged for letting a balance in another account slip.

Efficiency remained a problem. I kept accounts in the bank, both as a support and for research purposes, and I continued to have many frustrating experiences. These included closing out a checking account, and, subsequently, receiving month after month a statement reporting that I had a zero balance and zero activity. In the interest of saving the bank money (and fearing that I might be the tip of an iceberg), I tried to get it to stop sending statements. This error was particularly egregious in that management insisted that servicing low-balance accounts was a hindrance to making money, yet they went on providing service to a closed account. It took six months to get the statements stopped. Many customers had similar stories to tell.

Heagy's achievement at the bank was substantial, if not entirely successful. In the first years, he kept things afloat through his profitable activities in the bond market. In subsequent years, he oversaw the introduction of important new products in a period when the banking climate was undergoing dramatic change after deregulation. When the service charges he introduced later rose to an appropriate level, they became a major element in the bank's economic success. He laid the groundwork for a profitable bank in the future. He was unable, however, to straighten out operations. And, because of numerous changes in procedures and an assertive management style, he generated a great deal of uneasiness among bank personnel.

Although it was not part of his mandate, Heagy also laid the foundation for INDC's largest single development effort. He was able to persuade his former employer, the First National Bank, to participate in what was to become the 25 million dollar Parkside Project, which I will discuss in chapter 8.

Frustrated by his efforts to produce further satisfactory change and sensing that others were frustrated too, he resigned from the South Shore Bank in March 1980 to join a larger one downtown. Mary Houghton stepped in to fill the vacancy.

RAISING CAPITAL

Finding outside resources was not limited to bringing in new management. INDC was plagued by the continuous problem of finding capital. Having purchased the bank for $3.2 million with a $2,242,528 loan, INDC was faced with enormous interest expense that bank profits could not sustain. Federal bank examiners were also continually after the bank to improve its capital-to-asset ratios. Furthermore, the existing level of capitalization prevented INDC and the bank from carrying out its various activities.

The first big push in 1973–1974 resulted in raising $1,381,000 in equity capital. By 1978, that figure had climbed to $2,873,000 of common stock. Between 1980 and 1984, INDC sold another $2,416,250 of preferred stock, bringing the total capitalization to $5,289,250. During this same period, it was also able to sell $2,850,000 in long-term, interest-subsidized capital notes.

In retrospect, the figures appear both impressive and easily achieved. In fact, in those early days, it was difficult to sell INDC, an untried concept that seemed odd to many people. In addition, although located in a minority community, it was not, and is not, a minority-owned bank; for some people that was the litmus test of whether an investment or a deposit would be worthwhile.

With the exception of the courageous Wieboldt Foundation, led by Robert Johnson, Chicago foundations were very slow to get involved. Two local men with strong traditions of public concern, Edison Dick and Robert Lifton, were early Chicago investors. From the national level, the Center for Community Change, the New World Foundation, and the United Church of Christ Board of Homeland Ministries all played important early roles. Table 6.1 lists all of the shareholders as of March 1985. As can be seen, foundations across the entire United States are represented, as are a few unusual individuals.

As this book is being written, the bank once again has gone into the capital market. It is attempting to raise a $23,000,000 long-term development fund, $2,300,000 of which is earmarked for a new development effort in another Chicago neighborhood. Contrast this with the $800,000 with which it started.

BORROWING FOR DEVELOPMENT

Just as INDC had to turn away from South Shore, even Chicago, for its capital, it discovered that it had to do the same thing to improve its deposit base. It was increasingly clear to

Table 6.1

INDC Shareholders, March 1985

Albert Pick, Jr., Fund
Allstate Insurance Company
American Fletcher National Bank as Trustee
Amoco Neighborhood Development Company
Center for Community Change
CNA Financial
Cooperative Assistance Fund
Cummins Engine Foundation
Edison Dick
Eight South Fifty Four East, Inc. (Piton Foundation)
Episcopal Church of the USA
Carol Bernstein Ferry
Ford Foundation
Ronald Grzywinski
Harris Foundation
Irwin Sweeney Miller Foundation
Joyce Foundation
Robert Lifton
John D. and Catherine T. MacArthur Foundation
Henry Morgan
Charles Stewart Mott Foundation
New World Foundation
North Shore Unitarian Society
Shalan Foundation
South Shore Commission
Standard Oil of Indiana
Stern Fund
Telacu Investment Company
United Church of Christ Board of Homeland Ministries
Urban Investment and Development Company
Wieboldt Foundation
Woods Charitable Trust

management that its capacity to increase market share in South Shore was, at least for the time being, extremely limited. For whatever the reason—preferences for banking near one's place of work or another element of convenience, desire for better service or for prestige—market penetration was not improving. If the bank were to increase deposits, then, a more systematic effort had to be made to attract money from outside the community.

This effort had been made in the past. Bank officials met with large corporations and with religious groups that set aside money for savings and business accounts, as distinct from investment dollars, and that had met with some success in bringing their funds to the bank. One bank official argued that it was the development deposit dollars that kept the bank afloat in those early days. The decision was made to institutionalize the process.

Consequently, in 1974, Susan Davis, who had run a newsletter on women's rights and had tried to create a feminist magazine, was hired to develop a direct-mail campaign to solicit development deposits. She purchased early-generation electronic typewriters to grind out letters, purchased mailing lists, and ultimately participated in the production of glossy, bank annual reports to sell the product.

Because the quality of bank services was unreliable, the development deposit department took on the function of personal banker, handling deposits, withdrawals, and other transactions. Davis worked systematically to identify such groups as religious orders with charitable concerns, which controlled relatively large sums of money. The system of development deposits has continued to serve as the main resource for the bank's operating profits.

By year end 1986, the bank had deposits of $119 million. Forty-six million dollars were development deposits. That leaves $73 million, of which an unknown proportion were not, strictly speaking, local either. With inflation, the $38 million with which the bank started in 1973 would make them worth almost $94 million in today's market. This figure suggests that, despite a substantial marketing effort, massively improved services, and a somewhat more prosperous populace, the bank has not done well in its own market. However, it has been able to shift its deposit base from the small high-cost depositor to the larger and less expensive one. In this sense, its attractive new products and improved marketing did have an impact.

What is obvious is that the bank's development deposit program is essential to its operation because it provides an impor-

tant margin of profit. It does indeed receive adequate and continued attention.

BRINGING INVESTORS TO THE COMMUNITY

If it was clear to management from the early days that if
INDC were to succeed at making the bank profitable, it would
have to attract deposits and investments from the larger world,
it was equally clear that it would have to bring outside investors and developers into the community to achieve its development goals. Whatever the resources available in South Shore,
it seemed unlikely that they could provide the dramatic surges
necessary for South Shore to prosper.

So in mid-1974, bank management began a series of efforts
to attract outside capital to the community, while, at the same
time, they were looking for other points of entry to the problems within South Shore.

The most dramatic effort and, in some measure, achievement of this period involved Saul Klibanow. A former resident
of South Shore and past president of the South Shore Commission, Klibanow is a planner and architect, who headed an organization called RESCORP (Renewal Effort Service Corporation). Initially capitalized at $700,000, RESCORP is a consor-
tium of more than 50 savings and loan associations designed
to promote investment in risky inner-city projects as a means
of supporting redevelopment or of preventing urban decay.

RESCORP, newly minted in 1972, was looking for its first
project. Grzywinski and Davis set out to persuade Klibanow
that his old home, South Shore, was the place to put it. A
careful man, who was eager that his first effort be successful,
initially he leaned toward Rogers Park, a North Side city neighborhood that was in better condition than South Shore and
did not have its racial problems. The head of the Illinois Housing Development Authority (IHDA) was at that time a Hyde
Park resident and an old friend of Grzywinski's. Both of them
had worked in the successful gubernatorial campaign of Dan
Walker. Concerned about the future of the South Side, the
government official promised IHDA support to Klibanow if

he took on a South Side project, and intimated that IHDA would then be more forthcoming for other projects as well.

Klibanow was reluctant at first—he had been involved in the early commission effort to "save" South Shore and he was not sanguine about South Shore's future. He commissioned a study by a local real estate research organization to assess the future of the O'Keeffe area, a South Shore neighborhood. Tucked into the northeastern corner of the community, O'Keeffe is bounded by Jackson Park on the north, the South Shore Country Club on the east, Seventy-first Street, the area's main shopping strip, on the south, and Jeffrey, the street on which the South Shore Bank is located, is its western boundary. Primarily renter-occupied (85 percent), the O'Keeffe area was comprised mainly of three-story, walk-up apartments, many of which were courtyard buildings.

The Technical Assistance Corporation for Housing (TACH) engaged in a comprehensive study of the O'Keeffe area, concluding that "O'Keeffe is key in the destiny of the . . . South Shore area as a whole. . . . Total deterioration of the type that has been experienced by another South Shore rental neighborhood, Parkside, would undoubtedly influence South Shore's most stable and attractive single family neighborhoods. . . ." The report went on:

> Reversing trends of deterioration in urban neighborhoods has always involved significant risks and O'Keeffe is no exception. Such an endeavor is not for the timid. . . . Yet, if such improvements are delayed . . . one more opportunity to save an urban neighborhood may slip away.
>
> Housing rehab can serve as a catalyst for change, establishing a momentum that will result in a higher level of public and commercial services. To best assure that result, a massive, noticeable, and courageous rehabilitation program is called for. . . .
>
> O'Keeffe is not for the timid; however, for the concerned, inventive, courageous, and farsighted, it offers great potential.

The TACH recommendation of 1974 was adopted after a long period of negotiation. By the summer of 1976, RESCORP, with the assistance of IHDA and the federal Section 236 program, had spent approximately $3.7 million to rehabilitate 148 units of housing in eight buildings that had been carefully selected to make a significant impact on the surrounding units. Subsequently, RESCORP undertook rehabilitation of another 154 units for $4.2 million. These were completed by 1978.

The rehabilitation jobs were of high quality, with additional money spent for visible security arrangements. The U-shaped buildings, for example, were closed at their open ends with high black iron fencing, requiring that people be buzzed into the courtyard before being buzzed in again at each of the entryways. The apartments were popular, and management was able to select tenants, as many of the buildings had more applicants than apartments.

The RESCORP projects had spillover effects. During that period, an observer traveling through the community could see numerous other buildings undergoing some mode of rehabilitation after fairly long periods of neglect. It might be the addition of storm windows or a fresh tuck-pointing. It might be a new roof or a new entry system with improved security. Many of these projects were financed by the bank. It was unusual in South Shore, as it was in many communities of its type, to see the trucks of contractors in substantial numbers parked on the street. An area that formerly had seemed depressed had taken on new vitality.

That experience combined elements that were subsequently to be important in INDC planning. To begin with, RESCORP brought into the community an infusion of capital that the bank could never hope to provide. The bank was able to multiply its effects through lending to owners of nearby buildings. RESCORP's success also attracted others. The importance of such wide-ranging contacts such as those with IHDA was also underscored. Over time, INDC representatives came to work well with a variety of city, state, and federal agencies. It also became clear that making renovations near each other or near a point of strength was important in order to have maximum communitywide effects.

The bank, as a bank, was not idle during the 1974–1978 period. Management began to explore a program of making mortgages for multiple-family units. This was a step of some courage. There were no mortgages being made in South Shore by any source for those structures at that time, and, as I have said, the sorts of buildings that were in South Shore and the sort of neighborhood South Shore was perceived to be were understood to be prime sources of default and delinquency. In fact, some of the big real estate lenders in the Chicago area were still losing money on South Shore buildings.

More than that, it could be argued that making loans on multiple-family dwellings in a neighborhood that might decline is almost the equivalent of making unsecured loans. In an unambiguously appreciating neighborhood, this is not true. Many of the processes that work well in a stable or appreciating neighborhood can have peculiar repercussions in one on the skids. The best example relates to taxation policy. The threat of confiscation for nonpayment of taxes in an appreciating or stable area is usually enough to get the tax paid because the sale price of the building will be adequate to cover those costs and ensure some profit. Often, in a depreciating neighborhood, confiscation is not a threat, but a favor. It takes a difficult building off somebody's hands after he has not paid its taxes for some specified period of time. In this case, what looks punitive and clear-cut in good times has the effect of hastening precisely those problems good management usually seeks to avoid. But if the development process succeeds and if the lenders are good judges of character and situations, that activity, despite its risk, will have positive consequences for the neighborhood.

Management began to enter the mortgage lending business, albeit somewhat gingerly. Skills had to be developed to understand the buildings and their market. Bank management already felt that it could evaluate the character and quality of individuals who sought such mortgages. This was important, because lending judgments had to be made on whether plans for the building would realistically generate the revenues to cover costs rather than on its market value. They had an edge if the mortgage seeker lived in the building being purchased or, at least, nearby. Many of the buildings could not be made profitable unless the owner did much of the work, including repairs, rehabilitation, janitorial services, rent collection, and tenant selection himself or closely supervised those who did. If he lived in the building, he was more likely to take good care of it and pay careful attention to the others who lived there.

Similarly, it paid to force borrowers to rehabilitate their buildings or put money into escrow for maintenance and repairs as part of the mortgage contract. Many forms of federal subsidy and insurance required doing this, and where they did not, the bank tried to do it anyway. Since the bank was the only source of credit for such units, it was able to make tough demands and make them stick. By themselves, the sums placed in escrow could not realistically be expected to turn around undermaintained buildings. They did, however, communicate to prospective purchasers what was expected of them—to think about maintenance instead of milking and to plan for the longer term than building milkers normally do.

The requirement also worked as a screening device. To require some rehab or escrow deposit was equivalent to raising the rate of interest or monthly payments, and this provision substantially reduced a building's attractiveness to those interested in quick ghetto-type profits; it was acceptable only to those who wanted to make long-term investments and were looking for growth in equity capital. People unable to finance through South Shore Bank were forced either to purchase their buildings on contract, take a loan from the building's seller, or come up with the cash. Some managed to do each of these. Nonetheless, the proportion of total sales financed by South Shore, coupled with such redevelopment efforts as the RESCORP project, made a substantial impact. There were many people who wanted a building as a long-term investment, and even if the terms made them squirm, even if they felt that the requirements limited their freedom of action, and even if they objected to the paternalism of bank management, they could see the advantage to themselves in the long run.

The attraction, then, of RESCORP to the O'Keeffe area of South Shore as well as allied bank lending, marked an important turning point in the area's fortunes. That change is, in

Table 6.2

Negative and Positive Opinions about South Shore,
South Shore and O'Keeffe Residents Compared (Percentages)

Overall, has South Shore gotten better or worse during the past three or four years?

	O'Keeffe	Rest of South Shore
Better	23.0	12.8
The same	37.8	30.9
Worse	39.2	56.2

What do you think South Shore will be like in five years?

	O'Keeffe	Rest of South Shore
Better	60.0	34.7
The same	12.9	23.6
Worse	27.1	41.7

fact, measurable. In a 1978 survey, we asked residents about changes in South Shore over the preceding four years. In their answers to questions about South Shore's past and future, O'Keeffe residents were about twice as positive as the remainder of the community (see Table 6.2).

In chapter 7, I will discuss South Shore residents' perceptions of the future in comparison with the views of residents of other communities that underwent racial change during roughly the same period of time. What is evident is that all of the South Shore residents' perceptions of the recent past and future are more optimistic and positive than those in other communities with similar patterns of change. In that context, the optimism of the O'Keeffe residents is striking.

Developments in housing provided the fulcrum around which these views turned. In response to the question "What things do you think have improved in this neighborhood within the past three or four years?" 26.7 percent of O'Keeffe respondents spontaneously mentioned housing, as compared to 12.3 percent of the rest of South Shore. In response to the question "Has anything happened in the past three or four years that has had, or will have, a positive impact on South Shore?" the same percentage (although not always the same respondents), 26.7, spontaneously mentioned housing, as compared to 10.5 percent for the rest of South Shore.

In addition, residents were asked, "In the last three or four years, have any groups, governmental agencies, or businesses taken a new interest in South Shore?" Twenty-one point three percent of respondents in O'Keeffe answered this in the affirmative, as compared to 11.2 percent for the rest of the area.

This is a dramatic and measurable impact over a relatively short period of time. It should be added that the median income of the O'Keeffe area went up as well, as can be seen from Table 6.3. This increase took place with little or no displacement. The proportion of 1974 O'Keeffe residents still residing there in 1978 was higher than it was for South Shore as a whole.

RESCORP activities were not the only development-oriented events taking place in that area at that time. The bank was increasing the number of loans it was making in the area, and it was involved in the South Shore Villa project described below. Yet these data represent a dramatic demonstration of the enormous impact of well-planned housing development activity.

The bank commitment to aggressive rather than passive solicitation of loan requests continued in other activities as well. For example, bank officials decided in 1975 to target a stunning 39-unit, three-story, terra-cotta-and-white stone building with a large circular drive just across from the country club on South Shore Drive.

The decision was made to convert this striking and visible building to condominiums as a demonstration to developers

Table 6.3
Change in Median Family Income of South Shore Residents

Area	1974	1978
O'Keeffe	$10,908	$15,833
Rest of South Shore	10,758	12,356

that "black neighborhoods were ready for condominiums": that is, INDC management wanted to attack the conventional wisdom that it was hard to develop and sell condominiums in largely black neighborhoods. The view that such neighborhoods could not support condominiums seemed simply the product of prejudice by the real estate industry.

Because banks themselves are not allowed to invest directly in property not intended for their own use, management had to find a developer to undertake the conversion. When none was easily found, bank officials turned to two men, Grzywinski's brother, a man whose primary building experience had been in the construction and sale of suburban subdivisions, and a Hyde Park realtor. Because of its lending limits, the bank had to find a bank partner or two to help purchase the $500,000 building and to finance the rehabilitation. Again, because of traditional banking attitudes toward the area, the process required extensive negotiations and the concession from the bank that the financing partner come in on a last-in-first-out basis.

The deal was consummated, however, and the building converted, and although sales were not as quick as people had hoped, all of the units with mortgages provided by the South Shore Bank sold out within a year. The $975,000 of sales included a reasonable profit to its developers.

There is a sequel. Shortly after the building changed hands, a water main broke just in front of it, sending "5 million gallons of water rushing down the drive, disrupting utilities, damaging buildings and turning a 100-foot section of 69th Street into a gaping canyon that swallowed autos which had been parked along the curb" (*Chicago Sun-Times*, October 24, 1976).

One wall of the building was undermined and, consequently, cracked open. Because the building had been evacuated, vandals had the opportunity to break in and carry goods away. When the dust had settled, or rather, the water had dried up, condo owners found themselves with a major bill and a city reluctant to pay it. In addition, owners of some units lost so much to water damage and were so inadequately insured that they were unable to pay the costs of keeping their units. Only one, the purchaser who had made only a 10 percent down payment, defaulted, however.

CNA AND CHICAGO UNITED

In their efforts to bring more outside resources to South Shore, RESCORP and INDC began in early 1974 to meet with officials of the CNA Financial Foundation in order to put together a large program providing mortgage and other development moneys. CNA, a major insurance and other financial services company, was one of a group of companies associated with an organization called Chicago United. That organization was, and still is, a racially integrated association of some of Chicago's major corporations. The active members are people who have responsibility for community affairs, race relations, or a similar area in their corporations.

Klibanow of RESCORP had persuaded the community affairs vice president of CNA that a joint venture of Chicago's top corporations would be a dramatic demonstration project of the potential of such endeavors. The CNA vice president brought together officials from other major Chicago companies, representatives of the South Shore Bank, and such community residents as the president of the South Shore Commission for an almost year-long series of meetings to develop the program.

Ultimately, the concept of a $15 million development fund funneled through a group in which the South Shore Bank would be a major actor evolved, and the president, chief executive officer, and chairman of the board of CNA agreed to produce a slide show with a voice-over that could be carried from corporation to corporation. In fact, such a program was put together with the president of CNA making an impressive speech supported by pictures about why a neighborhood like South Shore was the appropriate place to conduct such a dramatic effort.

The truly amazing fact about this set of activities is that it took place as CNA was taking record financial losses, which were to lead to its takeover by a New York corporation. In October of 1974, they reported a loss of $145.6 million for the third quarter of the year, and a nine-month loss of $200.3 million (*Chicago Sun-Times*, October 31, 1974).

Cynical observers speculated about which would happen first, CNA's collapse or that of the South Shore Project. It was CNA by a hair. In December 1974, the president stepped down, and the company was taken over by Loew's. CNA's charitable and community-oriented arm was among the first to go in the bloodletting that followed. The story is illustrative for two reasons. The first is that, although the project seemed more grandiose than some, it demonstrates a process that was to continue and indeed continues to the present day—the funneling of resources into South Shore development from outside the community from some of America's corporate foundation giants. The second points out how decisions made downtown, or even elsewhere in the United States, can have measurable consequences on such a little place as South Shore. When we return to the problems of Seventy-first Street, we will see other examples. I will now turn to a more modest project, which, although also funded by an outside agency, helped bring bank services directly to residents.

THE PARKSIDE BANKER

The TACH report quoted earlier suggested that the neighborhood of Parkside was at that time the most deteriorated in South Shore. There were several reasons for its decline. The first was that it was the area that began the process of racial change earliest, and, unlike many places where the new residents are better off than those who are already there, many of its residents were not well off, but were trying to flee a particularly bad situation in Woodlawn. The new arrivals were property owners who thought they saw a good chance to purchase three-flat and six-flat houses and to build some equity, and lower-income renters. In addition, Parkside was also one of the few areas of South Shore where absentee landlords greedily milked their buildings.

Parts of Parkside were identified as a proposed urban renewal area that included parts of Woodlawn as well. The danger of announcing an area as slated for urban renewal is that it is a signal to property owners to stop investing in their property. The government will eventually purchase the property for a price of its own choosing, and the price varies little from improved to unimproved buildings. It makes little sense from the property owner's point of view to spend money on buildings that will not generate an adequate return. Substantial segments of Parkside began to run down as landlords waited for the government to purchase the property, clear it, and sell it at a reduced price to a developer.

The city, however, never followed through on its renewal plans for that area, and buildings were simply allowed to deteriorate. By the mid-1970s, the area was dotted with large run-down buildings, some of which were abandoned, others burned, and still others of which were tax-delinquent and clearly being milked.

The deteriorated buildings provided a contrast to the well-kept three- and six-flat ones of resident owners scattered about the area. These buildings had been purchased by their owners at the beginning of the racial change process, and although the owners had made substantial efforts to maintain their buildings, trying to rent only to relatives or close friends, their units were worth substantially less in the mid-1970s than in the sixties. They had scant market value. Nevertheless, many owners were proud of their buildings, worked hard to maintain them, and were moderately active in Parkside affairs. One was a member of the bank's citizens' advisory board. Somewhat angry at what had happened to her neighborhood, she was an articulate and thoughtful member of the board and was able to bring the plight of Parkside to the attention of bank management.

About that time, the bank was struggling to find ways to intercede in the process of decline—to move from being a passive agent waiting for people to bring them proposals to becoming a generator of redevelopment. One way would be to encourage residents to take loans to fix up their buildings.

Residents, however, made it clear that they were suspicious of the bank's avowed good intentions and were unwilling to get stuck once again in dealing with a bureaucracy that promised to deliver and then left things worse than they had been in the first place. If the buildings had little market value and the neighborhood was not going to upgrade, there was no point in investing in improvements.

Partly stimulated by an aggressive advertising campaign by a downtown bank for its "personal bankers," management hit on the idea of a series of subarea bankers who would focus their activities on the subareas, getting to know the owners and other residents personally in order to help them with their financial problems and to cultivate confidence. These positions could not be generated out of the bank's meager profits— the holding company was actually losing money—and, in the summer of 1976, foundation money was acquired for only one such position, for Parkside. Jim Bringley, the new Parkside banker, had come to the bank from Rochester, where he had worked in a city housing authority. A former Catholic seminarian, he had taken many administrative roles in the bank before coming to the Parkside position. In fact, he had been the most successful of the rotating managers responsible for dealing with the teller line problem. He was also developing expertise in real estate lending, particularly in South Shore, and in developing clear standards for making loans.

He set about his new position with characteristic energy. He met residents and looked over their properties with them, went to downtown records offices and developed good data on building ownerships and tax delinquencies, helped people get tax reductions on their property, assessed their needs, and proposed loan packages to them. The immediate result was twelve home improvement loans and one refinancing.

What he learned along the way was how deep Parkside's problems ran—that is, how many real problem buildings there were—and how uneasy the resident owners were about spending money on their buildings. Despite these odds, he did help generate loans and confidence in the bank in the area. Resident owners would ask for him when they had problems, and it was not long before other Parksiders joined the bank's citizens' advisory board. It became clear to Bringley and others, however, that if Parkside were to survive, it would take a massive intervention, far beyond the level of home improvement loans to the small property owners.

That massive intervention was to occur, and I will discuss it in some detail in chapter 7. It is important to note at this time that, because the bank had the small building owner's confidence, when the infusion of outside funds took place, it did so with surprisingly little disruption to the area.

THE PHOENIX PARTNERSHIP

As it became increasingly clear that positive developments were taking place in housing, particularly in the O'Keeffe area north of Seventy-first Street, it was also becoming clear that Seventy-first Street itself was a serious and almost intractable problem. Shopping strips have special problems in neighborhoods that are either undergoing racial change or have recently gone through the process. There are several reasons.

The first is that shopping strips in city neighborhoods function something like the main streets of small towns. They serve as symbols of the community as a whole. People driving through city neighborhoods are most likely to do it on the city's major thoroughfares, and what they see on the strip is what they think of the community. In the change process, nowhere is the expectation that things will go downhill as strong a self-confirming prophecy as what happens on these strips. Any signs of deterioration are seized upon by observers as evidence that matters have already begun their downward trajectory. We have documented elsewhere (Taub, Taylor, and Dunham, 1984) the fact that overt occurrences that in strong neighborhoods are interpreted positively are more likely to be interpreted negatively in neighborhoods perceived to be changing. Nothing panics people who are worried about the future of their community more than a vacant storefront—except perhaps a boarded-up building. Yet, it is in the nature of things that some small businesses will fail over time, anywhere. In a neighborhood with a strong economic future, an empty store is evidence either that the former owner was a poor business-man, or that he just died, or that he could no longer afford the rents in an improving area.

The same empty storefront in a racially changing neighbor-hood is perceived as evidence that the neighborhood is in de-cline. Neighborhood development corporations, therefore, often focus on their strips as key problems to deal with.

This is particularly important because shopping strips in general have had a difficult time succeeding in the late 1970s and 1980s. To begin with, their stores are outmoded. They draw from too small an area and they have too few square feet. Their owners are undercapitalized, and the selection of merchandise is not very large. Finally, the driving conditions are usually congested in such areas, and parking is a prob-lem. This set of deficiencies is important because of the im-plicit comparison it makes with what is available both in shopping centers and downtown. Shopping centers provide parking, large modern stores with nationally advertised brands, and large selections of merchandise. They are able to do so at somewhat lower prices than neighborhood shops can. They bring customers in with big organized promotions. And, of course, shopping centers draw customers from substan-tially larger areas than a single neighborhood. In a world of two-earner families where free time is scarce, the shopping center, with its one-stop easy-parking shopping, is a special attraction.

Under those circumstances, for a neighborhood strip to do well, it must offer something special. It may be that it is located in the core of an ethnic neighborhood where the shop-keepers speak the language and carry large quantities of spe-cialized merchandise. Aside from those more obvious attrac-tions, it is probably also true that there are arrivals from the old country who simply feel more comfortable in a store that gives personal service and where gossip is exchanged than in a large, glossy, and impersonal one.

Some ethnic neighborhoods may then become attractions for tourists as well as the inhabitants, as their exotic wares bring outsiders from all over. Chinatowns are obvious examples. Similarly, gentrifying neighborhoods with boutiques and lots of restaurants for singles and young two-earner couples who find it easier to eat out often than to cook at home may begin to attract a citywide clientele for their specialties.

But where special attractions do not exist, it is difficult to maintain the old strips. In 1973, South Shore had 1,200 storefronts for a population of 80,000. Even a freestanding city of that size with fewer nearby competitors would have half as many stores.

The point is that even if South Shore had not been undergoing change, many stores would have failed. That has happened in other neighborhoods in the city. But when they failed in South Shore, it was taken as a sign that the neighborhood was on the skids.

Black neighborhood shopping strips in the 1970s and 1980s have other forces working against them as well. The first is that, unlike the ethnics who feel more comfortable in their own stores, black people do not particularly like to shop in their own communities. Blacks often have the feeling, which is based on a certain historical reality, that black neighborhoods get inferior merchandise. Indeed, there have been times and places when supermarket chains shipped their poorest wares to ghetto stores, and where retail establishments charged customers more for less (Caplowitz, 1967).

And then there is, as I have mentioned, the well-documented, extra-strong attraction to nationally advertised brand names, which arises from generations of feeling second-class.

If the above were not enough, there are the unemployed troublesome youths who stand on street corners and say threatening and uncomfortable things to passersby. They function as a deterrent to window-shopping and to leisurely strolls down the street. In fact, such pockets of young men make people so uncomfortable or fearful that they stay away from those streets altogether.

Therefore shopping strips anywhere, but particularly in predominantly black neighborhoods, are difficult, perhaps impossible, to revitalize. The reasons for the failure of these strips extend far beyond the simple lack of available credit or other problems related directly to discrimination. They extend to large-scale developments in the retail business that have little to do with either South Shore or with the problems of racial change.

The bank management did not necessarily know this when it began its own efforts. One clear strategy in the early period was to make loans available to promising business people in South Shore. I have already discussed the story of Conrad Brown in chapter 2. There were also shopkeepers along the strip who seemed energetic, imaginative, and innovative. With experience in their businesses and knowledge of their particular clientele, they seemed to be just the sort of people to support. In no case, however, have they been able unambiguously to succeed. In most cases they failed lugubriously. Two stores did survive longer than the rest. One was owned by an imaginative woman who sold women's clothing and accessories. Unlike most of the other efforts, which failed within the first two years, her business lasted for more than ten years. She found herself, however, unable to match rising expenses with rising profits, decided it was all too much, and gave up.

The other was a quasi-franchised gift shop, which was started in the mid-1970s with a substantial bank loan. To help that project get off the ground, one bank officer spent almost quarter-time for a year planning and making arrangements. This store, too, continued in business for about ten years, barely producing income for its owner. In January of 1985 it was hanging by a thread.

The bank also promoted and staffed the growth of a local development corporation, a citizens' group that had the legal capacity to lend out Small Business Administration funds at a subsidized rate. Its main achievement was to subsidize the purchase of a supermarket (which its members hoped would be a classy one) after one of the national chains had closed its doors. That market, alas, did not live up to its promise. But it represented an important development in South Shore, where at least four chains had once been represented with nine stores, and where there was then only one left, and that at the edge of the community.

One other set of developments should be mentioned. First, in 1977 one of the big supermarket chains, National Tea, considered opening a store on Seventy-first Street across from the South Shore Country Club. To do so involved buying up all the buildings on one block and tearing them down. Most of the buildings were simple storefronts. But one was a multiple-story building, which in the 1960s had been an important medical office building.

There was some opposition from the community to both tearing down the buildings and the specific new use to which the land would be put—that is, a supermarket with a large parking lot and much traffic. Indeed, this was another situation in which the bank supported a development activity in the face of community opposition. The process continued, however. National Tea made the purchase, and tenants were evicted.

The day after it made the purchase, however, National Tea announced from its office in one of Chicago's suburbs that it was closing all of its stores in the city. Both National Tea and South Shore were stuck with one of the neighborhood's prime business blocks, tenantless and undermaintained.

A tenantless block is a terrible depressant. Windows break in the storefronts. Derelicts stand in recessed doorways. Litter collects, sometimes swirling about in the wind. Studies of litter on shopping strips show that it always collects in front of vacant stores (Wittberg, 1982). The difference between a clean street and a dirty one is not so much the habits of the pedestrians or the quality of city services, but rather the zeal of shopkeepers who sweep the sidewalk around their stores every morning.

That property has been a depressant ever since. National Tea sold it, the new owners did not have the resources to make improvements, and the buildings were demolished. Seventy-first Street lives with a classic example of the consequences of the fact that decisions made outside the community can have an enormous impact on what takes place inside it. This is true even when those decisions are made not for malevolent or racial reasons, but because of general business incompetence.

It also illustrates a continuing problem of doing development in an area perceived to be on the decline. If Seventy-first Street were a hot property, National Tea could have turned around and quickly sold it to a well-capitalized developer. Nobody would have noticed that an error had been made. But National Tea was stuck with a property nobody else with real resources wanted, and ultimately, it had to sell under terms that were undesirable, to people who could not afford it and who hoped to make a profit through a quick resale.

It was in this context, then, that the Phoenix Partnership represented an important development. It was an effort by a group of investors in 1976 to buy up three blocks on the north side of Seventy-first Street, and to try to coordinate development activities so that there would be sufficient impact on all the stores at once: noticeable renovation, new stores, and shared promotions, which would generate customer traffic for all of them.

The organizer of the project was Steve Perkins. He held a Ph.D. in psychology from the University of Chicago and had served as executive director of the Hyde Park Kenwood Community Conference. In the early days of the INDC, he had served as public relations and marketing director of the South Shore Bank. During that time, he organized the start-up of the bank's drive-in facility. He then left Chicago briefly, only to return with the idea of fixing up a long stretch of Seventy-first Street through an investment company, which became the Phoenix Partnership.

Borrowing about $250,000 from the bank, the corporation purchased three blocks of buildings, which housed 35 storefronts on the north side of Seventy-first Street. Initially enthusiastic, bank managers had entered into the purchase reluctantly. It seemed high-risk, and they were not sure about the qualifications of all the partners—particularly those who were to get professional fees for their participation. They knew

Perkins and were involved personally with him, but banking traditions require "arm's-length" dealings, so doing business with Perkins under these circumstances represented an ambiguous case.

On the other hand, Perkins was full of ideas and enthusiasm. By purchasing a whole block of stores, he thought that he could set a consistent tone, seeing that all renters were up to his standards and that maintenance was kept at the proper level. A revitalized block could have real impact.

He planned to create specialized groups of stores. For example, a children's area would include a children's shoe store, a clothing store, and a store that specialized in both giving birthday parties and selling party supplies. He thought that if he could develop clusters like that, he could generate real traffic. He thought that he could push out the second-class renters— people who sold cheap merchandise in inner-city neighborhoods (for example, wig shops)—and project an image of class. The architect on his team had ideas about how to redo storefronts in an impressive but inexpensive fashion. Perkins was going to hire somebody to help recruit merchants to the area.

The enthusiasm and level of commitment as well as the intelligent planning were impressive indeed. After much hesitation and negotiation, the bank agreed to the deal. Later, when it became clear the project would not succeed, Perkins would attribute part of its failure to the bank's reluctant and inadequate level of financial participation.

As I said, the project did not succeed. Despite some impressive starts—some storefront renovation and a few new attractive tenants—the group could never get enough good tenants so that each would serve as a magnet. One good store standing alone, with insufficient parking, empty storefronts nearby, the litter, and the troublemaking youths, was not sufficient to generate profitable business and change the fortune of the block.

There were heartening signs and activities along the way. Milton Davis, Perkins, and Ronald Grzywinski persuaded the city to spend $750,000 rehabilitating the sidewalk area, planting young trees and putting some attractive brickwork around them. The project took a long time to get under way. There was not enough money to do all of Seventy-first Street. So merchants along the strip were vying with one another to get the improvements in front of their stores. Finally, those matters were resolved, and Seventy-first Street had an attractive new sidewalk. Similarly, there were times when it looked as if the Phoenix Partnership would take hold. There was talk of numerous potential tenants, and the occasional new tenant would arrive with impressive credentials, and sometimes even a fine store emerged. Perkins and his group sought extensions and additional loans from the bank. The bank's own ambivalence, however, was reinforced by pressure from federal bank examiners, who did not think it was a very good loan.

In 1981, the bank wrote off part of its loan to Phoenix Partnership, and the relationship ended with bad feelings on both sides. Perkins felt that he had not received adequate financial support from the bank. (The bank provided the loan for purchase; the conflict was over the level of support for rehabilitation and staffing.) Bank management did not think Perkins had done as well as he might have. The Phoenix project does not represent the end of efforts on Seventy-first Street, though. I shall discuss the more recent initiatives in a subsequent chapter.

It should be added that, although all three of the main shopping strips in South Shore—Seventy-fifth Street and Seventy-ninth Street are the other two—are in more or less equally bad shape, there is indirect evidence that at least part of the problem stems more from the inadequacy of old-fashioned shopping strips than from mismanagement. That evidence is found along Stony Island Avenue, the western boundary of the community. Once a beat-up strip with used-car lots, warehouses, and small manufacturers, it now contains branches of large chain stores, which advertise extensively and provide free parking in spacious open lots.

Zayre, a low-price general merchandise company; one of Jewel's giant supermarkets; and Calumet Meats, a mass-production retail market, are all thriving. Although they are located on the edge of South Shore, these stores draw on a much larger market. Stony Island Avenue is a major north-south artery and, consequently, large numbers of potential customers pass the stores daily.

The older communities with outdated stores and inadequate facilities pay a price for the process of change. There is almost no quantity of resources that will convert most of the strips to profitability. The empty stores and those with second-class uses stand as a symbol of decay that may screen the fact of vitality in the rest of the community.

SUMMARY

Some of the events reported here have been compressed in time in order to improve clarity. The important thing to note, however, is that after a first year in which initiatives seemed sporadic and bank development efforts limited and not, on balance, dramatically successful, new management had begun to take hold. Many of its big achievements involved bringing outside resources to the community. Its most successful efforts in the development area were attracting outside capital for RESCORP's project in O'Keeffe and the development of South Shore Villa. The Parkside Banker program, subsidized by an outside foundation, laid the groundwork for future development efforts. Capital growth was impressive. And the development deposit program began to build a channel that would successfully bring other outside resources into the community. Let us now turn in more detail to INDC's important achievements.

7

Achievements— The Bank's First Six Years

Before I show how the Illinois Neighborhood Development Corporation came to reorganize itself in order to deliver real development, on the one hand, and make enough of a profit to encourage others to try, on the other, it is time to step back and note INDC's achievements up to that point. They are important, because the almost inevitable focus on problems does deflect attention from achievements. The INDC may not have been delivering the goods most efficiently, but it had been delivering the goods; and in an environment which was not particularly supportive.

The point is that through 1978, INDC and its bank had survived and had done so while devoting substantial resources to development activity and carrying a large burden of debt. This achievement has to be placed in context.

First of all, the atmosphere for inner-city banking during this period seemed not very encouraging. I have already reported that many experts had predicted that the bank would fail. Indeed, that was what was happening to banks on the South and West sides of Chicago. Two banks in the South Shore area also failed during this period, despite the fact that each had substantial institutional support of sorts and no costly development agenda. Banking authorities offered South Shore Bank the opportunity to buy both banks. Each, however, had a negative net worth. One was headed by one of Mayor Daley's favorite black politicians—a former Notre Dame basketball star and a ward committeeman—who was able to get city deposits as a form of subsidy, and the other was controlled by the Black Muslims, whose economic fortunes seemed to wax and wane.

The only other South Side bank in a minority neighborhood within the city of Chicago that showed a strong profit position was one that simply collected deposits and invested the money elsewhere. Like a huge vacuum cleaner, it soaked up available funds and invested them in Iowa and Texas. Its management explained that they did not make mortgages because banks do not make mortgages (savings and loan institutions do that), and it did not invest in other ways, because there were no investment opportunities in their kind of neighborhood. Such assertions are common to banks like this.

In addition, the city's two largest savings and loan associations opened branches in the immediate area. With their immense advertising capacity and higher general level of prestige, they had the potential to attract depositors from South Shore and away from the bank.

Another way to understand this period and to evaluate the South Shore Bank's performance is to compare it with black-owned banks on a national basis. An analysis of the literature by Cole and his colleagues (1985) suggests that black banks are "less profitable and significantly different in asset and liability composition from their non-black counterparts" (p. 31), with particular problems in high loan loss rates, high liquidity, and low loan-to-deposit ratios (p. 39). It follows that their record in economic development is not impressive. By contrast, South Shore Bank had managed to maintain a high loan-to-deposit ratio.

During this period, then, of a difficult business environment, the South Shore Bank survived, and it did so respectably. Although it was often in the bottom quarter of banks in Illinois in terms of profitability, it was never at the very bottom. Its successes were sometimes due to pulling rabbits out of hats—

Table 7.1

South Shore Bank Year-End Figures, 1973–1985

(in thousands of dollars)

Year	Assets	Deposits	Loans	Net Operating Income or Loss[a]	Net Income	Stock-holders' Equity
1973	$44,200	$40,600	$16,200	$160	$159	$2,800
1974	41,536	35,623	21,088	(86)	(283)	2,553
1975	42,979	39,107	23,461	100	194	2,747
1976	54,506	48,101	24,891	165	429	3,119
1977	65,607	59,549	29,711	222	424	4,003
1978	76,972	57,360	36,815	120	208	4,070
1979	76,257	64,806	46,958	273	301	4,301
1980	81,957	75,435	50,388	351	432	4,347
1981	80,859	72,982	54,596	117	36	4,877
1982	86,408	77,031	59,320	131	48	6,174
1983	103,660	95,114	60,506	841	847	6,468
1984	106,317	95,937	68,169	1,053	663	6,832
1985	120,072	110,450	77,553	1,925	1,263	7,650

[a] Less security gains, taxes, and extraordinary items.

such as earning money in the bond market, as I have discussed; or saving money by leaving the national bank system and becoming a state bank; making loans on hospital equipment purchased by leasing companies—nonetheless, it survived, and its capital structure continued to improve as its successes made it more attractive to socially concerned investors (see Table 7.1).

If the business environment were not particularly encouraging, the same could be said for the regulatory structure in which the bank had to operate. In the early 1970s, banks were supposed to be investing in their communities, and were, at least in theory, supported in this endeavor by regulatory authorities. The Community Reinvestment Act (CRA) required them to report what level of investment they were making in their deposit areas, and, although this was mainly a potential lever for activist community groups, it was supposed to be part of the bank examination as well.

Examiners, however, cannot get into serious trouble if the banks they examine fail to invest in the community. But they can if they neglect to point out signs of difficulty that might lead to failure. Similarly, banks may get their hands slapped by examiners for failing to invest in their community, although in fact, this seldom happens; but they face serious penalties if they do not measure up to the financial standards of the examiners. In the South Shore context, this meant that examiners were looking for bad loans, adequate loan loss reserves, and those key ratios such as capital-to-assets that help determine a bank's future solvency. It was just fine that the bank was a development bank, but the real issue was, How did the loans look? There's the rub. In some sense, many development loans will look questionable to examiners. If there had been no ambiguity about the status of such investments, aspiring local businessmen would have been able to get money from a variety of other sources.

In the short run, at least, a bank is not going to fail because it does not make loans in its community. The long run may be a different matter. If a bank can contribute to strengthening the community, it may have a stronger and better depositor base in the future and may be able to make better loans to expanding businesses rather than to start-ups. But prospects are much too vague for the examiner, who wants to know whether the bank will succeed or fail in the near term. Examiners are likely to get particularly tough in settings where nearby banks have been failing and doing so dramatically.

They may also get tough if it seems that the bank is taking unnecessary risks not only with its development loan portfolio, but also in its efforts to make more money in other ways. For example, in order to earn a bigger return on bond investments, the bank moved some proportion of its portfolio from triple-A-rated investments to some with a BAA rating. There is evidence that threat of failure was very little more than it was with triple-A bonds, but the ratings are made on the internal economic structure of the corporations floating the bonds, and, in some experts' judgments, they are better vehicles than the others. The perception of risk is what raises the interest rates, producing more income to the bank. That same perception of risk makes bank examiners nervous. The same might be true of loans made outside the community for programs that carry unusually high interest rates or fees.

Therefore, the bank must not only succeed in doing business in a hostile business environment, it must operate in a regulated context in which the regulators do not care very much about the bank's avowed goals. The need to protect the bank's depositors and insurers from risk pushes examiners in a conservative direction. In addition, their guidelines come from the same banking world that has traditionally turned off the flow of credit to communities like South Shore.

Consequently, if an organization is committed to the process of development in a setting where traditional standards have led to disinvestment, its guidelines are not necessarily those of the examiners. Obviously, such a position is a difficult one for a bank. As good aggressive bankers should, South Shore management fought with examiners to try to get them to see things their way, and sometimes they succeeded. In the meantime, management spent a great deal of time on the road, rounding up more capital to strengthen the bank's foundation while reducing the load of indebtedness generated by the initial bank purchase.

Survival would not be enough to justify the bank's existence. The boards of directors of both the bank and INDC would not have been satisfied with that. What is impressive about the board is that it provided prudent encouragement at almost every step down the risky path. What is impressive about the bank is that during this period of uncertain profits and some harassment from examiners, the bank continued to do development lending.

Table 7.2 shows the volume of real estate lending between the years 1974 and 1978. It must be noted that these loans were made in an area that was, for all intents and purposes, redlined before the new management arrived.

For real estate alone, then, in this period, the bank had lent $11,594,000. If we assume that each of those loans required a 20 percent down payment (reasonable down-payment require-

Table 7.2

South Shore Bank Real Estate Loans

Year	Single-family	Multi-family	Home Improvement
1974	$ 891,000	0	0
1975	1,509,000	0	$ 310,000
1976	1,314,000	$ 102,000	322,000
1977	1,596,000	949,000	398,000
1978	1,619,000	1,748,000	836,000
Total	$6,929,000	$2,799,000	$1,866,000

ments for real estate purchases), there are investments in South Shore property of almost $14 million.

The bank made other contributions to real estate development as well. For example, there was the $750,000 expenditure the city made on Seventy-first Street. In addition, RESCORP's New Vistas project had cost $8 million. In 1976, the South Shore Area Development Corporation, staffed by bank personnel, loaned $250,000 in SBA funds for the purchase and improvement of a former chain supermarket building. There had also been a project, organized by Mary Houghton in 1977 and led by community residents, to rehabilitate with subsidies a small string of row houses, which cost $200,000. Throughout this period, the major Chicago newspapers ran articles about the exciting developments in South Shore. At one point, I had counted more than 200 positively oriented column inches about the area and the bank's role.

These development efforts directly bore fruit. A study conducted by the Woodstock Institute reported substantial property appreciation in single-family homes during this period (Woodstock, 1982). My study of changing property values, which compared rates of change to those of other communities comparable in some respects, showed real relative growth.

If one compared South Shore to areas which had gone through the racial change process at a similar time, the differences were particularly dramatic. Table 7.3 illustrates com-

Table 7.3

*Change in Median Sale Price of Detached
Single-Family Houses, 1973–1978*

Community	1973	1978	Increase (percent)
South Shore	$22,900	$45,000	96
Portage Park	33,000	64,000	95
East Side	25,000	41,000	64
Austin	20,000	31,000	55
Back of the Yards	17,000	20,250	19

Source: Taub, Taylor, and Dunham, *Paths of Neighborhood Change.* (Chicago: University of Chicago Press, 1984). © 1984 by the University of Chicago, reprinted with permission.

parative pricing changes for single-family houses in a group of selected neighborhoods.

Comparison with each of the communities in Table 7.3 provides some special insights. Consider each community separately. The Austin community most nearly parallels South Shore on racial matters. It, too, began the racial change process in the 1960s. Much larger in both area and population (125,000 as compared to 80,000) and with a smaller proportion of multi-family dwellings, it had not gone as far in the change process as South Shore had. Nonetheless, its levels of property appreciation were 57 percent as high as South Shore's. I already noted in chapter 3 that for five years prior to 1973, property value in South Shore was scarcely appreciating.

Portage Park was selected originally as an all-white, non-changing community with original property values comparable to South Shore's. Matching communities is a difficult matter. Portage Park was more of a lower-middle-and working-class community than South Shore was in the days when its residents were mainly white, and somewhat more Eastern European in its ethnicity. In addition, its proportion of single-family housing was larger than South Shore's, and that fact has some impact on pricing dynamics. Nonetheless, in the late 1960s and early 1970s its property appreciation was more than double that of South Shore's. In the subsequent period, South Shore caught up.

The other two communities represent interesting comparison points, although one should be careful not to make too much of either.

Like South Shore, East Side is located in the steel mill area. Unlike South Shore's, its residents at the time reported in this study were mainly white people of predominantly Eastern European descent, although there was a sprinkling of people with Mexican origins as well. Also, unlike South Shore, whose residents worked mainly downtown, the fortunes of East Side were very closely tied to the steel industry, which for the period under consideration had been in continuous decline in the region. Although in many respects a pleasant ethnic community, East Side is not a particularly attractive place with distinctive amenities or convenience of location. Consequently, its lack of property appreciation had relatively little to do with race and more to do with the declining economic opportunities for the residents of the area.

Finally, as can be guessed from the table, Back of the Yards has always been a much poorer area than South Shore, with its declining fortunes tied to what had once been the famous stockyards. During the time under consideration, its population consisted in about equal thirds of primarily aging white ethnics of Eastern European origins, a substantial and growing Mexican-American population, and a growing black population.

The point of all this is that, placed in this sort of neighborhood context, South Shore was doing surprisingly well. There were, however, other areas of the city at this time where property was appreciating at substantially higher rates. Nonetheless, the comparison areas provided here are as close to appropriate as one is likely to find.

Coupled with this property appreciation, community residents also were more optimistic about the future of their neighborhood than were the residents of comparable neighborhoods, and they became more optimistic over the period being studied.

Table 7.4

*Improvement or Decline of Neighborhoods as Seen
by Their Members (percentage)*

Community	Better	About the Same	Worse
South Shore	16.6	44.6	38.8
Austin	8.5	48.4	43.0
Back of the Yards	8.2	46.5	45.3
East Side	14.2	68.8	17.0
Portage Park	6.8	82.6	10.6

In 1979, residents in these same communities were asked how their community had fared in the past two years and how they thought things would be in the next two (see Table 7.4). Although South Shore residents could not be characterized as wildly enthusiastic about either the past or the future, they did report a measure of optimism.

The table shows that South Shore residents were somewhat more content with changes in their neighborhood than were residents of other communities which had either gone through racial change or were still in the process. Although the optimistic numbers are still small, they are twice as great for South Shore as they are for the other two racially changing communities: that is, Austin and Back of the Yards. I must point out that in all three changed or changing communities, there is a substantial minority that felt things had gotten worse. This is particularly true in comparison to the other two white communities presented here. As I have discussed, blacks in recently changed communities often feel worse about what has happened to their communities than whites do. They assume that things are going downhill and will continue to do so. South Shore's modestly more positive evaluation of the recent past as compared to the other black communities was positive, but not decisive in important ways.

These differences, however, become more notable when the respondents evaluated how things were likely to be in the next two years (see Table 7.5).

Table 7.5

Inhabitants' Predictions of Community Conditions for Next Two Years, 1978–1980 (percentage)

Community	Better	About the Same	Worse
South Shore	35.8	35.1	29.1
Austin	17.3	39.5	43.0
Back of the Yards	14.4	40.4	45.1
East Side	10.1	73.4	16.5
Portage Park	10.0	74.1	15.9

Table 7.5 dramatically demonstrates two important points. The first is that South Shore residents were substantially more optimistic about their future than were the residents of the other two changing communities. (It should be pointed out that in all three communities, black residents alone either ranked their communities in the same way whites do or they were more pessimistic.)

Indeed, the levels of optimism for a Chicago community in South Shore's racial plight were unparalleled. On the other hand, the white communities were still substantially less likely than the mostly black ones to see a decline in the future. Given the low levels of property appreciation in East Side and the state of the steel industry (whose position was somewhat more ambiguous at the time of this survey), the residents of that neighborhood probably had unrealistically placed themselves in the "about the same" category.

It is not easy to demonstrate that these developments are the effect of INDC investment activity. There are other possible explanations. It does, however, seem to be the best way to account for both the real changes in investment levels in the community and the relative optimism of its residents.

It was increasingly clear that things had to change on two levels if INDC were to have continuous and growing impact on the community. The first was that the bank would have to become more profitable and achieve that profitability on a stable basis, for it was only with sufficient bank profitability that INDC would have the resources to continue and to expand its efforts in the community.

Second, it was clear that the INDC had to become more aggressive in its development efforts. Lending and encouraging people to borrow are virtually the only weapons a bank has in its arsenal to encourage development activity. New ways had to be found for the parent corporation to work toward development goals.

Let me turn now to the reorganization of the bank and the creation of new components of the Illinois Neighborhood Development Corporation, for it was with renewed efforts to reorganize the bank and with the creation of new subsidiaries and affiliates that INDC began to move forward in a solid and assured fashion.

8

Reorganization for Attack

The 1978–1980 period was the turning point for INDC. The bank was reorganized in such a way that it could begin to produce real profits, and the holding company was reorganized with new subsidiaries, which could enter into the development process more definitively than any had in the past. Taking advantage of a little-known law about bank holding companies and reverting to Grzywinski's original proposal, INDC created two new subsidiaries and an "affiliate." These included a for-profit real estate development subsidiary, City Lands Corporation, designed to purchase real estate, renovate it, and sell it to private investors; a Minority Enterprise Small Business Investment Company (MESBIC); The Neighborhood Fund (TNF); and a not-for-profit socially oriented agency, The Neighborhood Institute (TNI), which was to help neighborhood groups identify their special needs and then organize activities to achieve them.

In this chapter, I will discuss the most important features of the reorganization: the development of a talented middle-management cadre and efficient day-to-day procedures at the bank while staff size was being reduced, the creation of TNI, and the development of City Lands. Because it has not played much of a role in specifically South Shore developments, I will not discuss The Neighborhood Fund.

BANK REORGANIZATION

When Tom Heagy left the bank in 1980, Mary Houghton stepped in to help sharpen operations. With outside advice, she, along with other top management, began aggressively to construct a strong and experienced middle-management cadre to take over day-to-day operations.

They identified the talented nonknowers within the bank and brought them into the management decision-making processes for the first time. With so much focus by the leaders of the bank on development activity, it had seemed very difficult for the bank to grow its own operations people. But there were promising young managers, who, with nurture and support, began to develop.

New outside managers whose skills complemented those of the insiders were hired. For example, a manager from a Hyde Park bank who was also a South Shore resident was brought in to take charge of operations, and one of the promising younger people in operations was given increased responsibility to bring order into the bank's operations. Similarly, a new director of commercial lending, with experience in the Small Business Administration, was added to the staff.

Two former University of Chicago graduate students—one joined the bank staff as a sociological fieldworker and the other initially signed on to support himself while he did graduate work in English—began to demonstrate useful skills. The sociologist became a lender and was involved particularly in locating profitable loan opportunities. The English literature student, who had been working part-time in the comptroller's office, was ultimately promoted to comptroller.

As new units were created to take on development responsibility outside the bank, management decided to close the bank's own development division—"everything we do should be development"—and to reduce staff size, particularly at the upper-middle levels. At that time, the bank was operating with about 50 percent more staff members than banks of comparable size, but some of that difference in size was justified by the nature of the bank and its operations.

First, the bank was involved in development lending. Development loans took up a great deal of time. Lenders often worked closely with potential borrowers showing them how to prepare the right financial statements and business plans as well as how to deploy their assets. In some instances, they provided consultation as well. Development activity was not profitable in a normal bank. But, the argument went, it was necessary to do it in South Shore, and the costs would be borne by development depositors, those people outside the community who had put their money into the bank in order to foster development.

Similarly, as we have seen, it was argued that lower-income customers with limited experience with financial institutions in general had special needs and consequently required more services than did more sophisticated, better-off individuals. Special services were provided: for example, at one point, the bank gave mini-courses in how to balance a checkbook.

As time went on, however, and the bank's profits did not match its aspirations, these services became luxuries. The crass reality was that the bank was overstaffed, in the higher as well as lower reaches of management. The process of divestment of upper-middle management was begun in a slow and careful way: that is, employees were encouraged to look elsewhere. In some instances, they were provided with outplacement services while remaining, at least nominally, in their positions. Under those circumstances, it took more than a year to reduce the staff enough to produce results for the bottom line.

Throughout the early 1980s, the bank continued to market itself forcefully, aiming at the more affluent depositor. The Prestige Account department discussed earlier took definite shape, with a clear package of services, including a special teller window with short lines, and a new staff member whose responsibility was to untangle bureaucratic problems. For example, I wished to have my pay check deposited automatically in the bank. The first effort to do so failed, and the check was forwarded from the bank to my house. The Prestige Account manager arranged to have checks sent directly to her so that she might deposit them.

By early 1985, there were approximately 2,500 such accounts in the bank, with an average balance of $6,400. New certificates of deposit programs and other bundled packages evolved as well. Service charge policy, which had begun with ambivalence because it seemed to run against the bank's mission, was applied more stringently in order to cover costs. Today, many of South Shore's service charges are as high as any in the area and are an important source of bank income. In 1985, they accounted for about $1,500,000 of revenue.

Having smoothed out many of the rough edges in bank operations, in 1983 Houghton moved into the holding company to work with Grzywinski on plans for INDC expansion. She was replaced by Jim Fletcher in order to consolidate operational achievements. Fletcher had been part of the original team, along with Grzywinski, Davis, and Houghton at the Hyde Park Bank. He did not come with the others to South Shore, but instead headed a MESBIC for the holding company that also owned the Hyde Park Bank. He joined INDC in 1978 to head the newly founded Neighborhood Institute, which I will discuss below. One of his accomplishments in the bank was to use consultants who could demonstrate how to cut costs further and improve efficiency through staff reduction and technology. The result was enhanced profitability.

THE NEIGHBORHOOD INSTITUTE

One of the most striking innovations of the whole INDC endeavor was the creation of The Neighborhood Institute as a not-for-profit affiliate.

The institute was conceived as a solution to two problems that the bank and its other affiliates faced as for-profit organizations. The first is that because banks must show a profit, they are unable to use their resources for the "softer" aspects of development: community mobilization, tenants' rights advocacy, job training and education, putting pressure on the schools to perform, and insisting on the delivery of social services. Yet, if a group wants to have a positive influence in development, this component must be part of the total process.

Second, there are foundations willing to support such activities. The law, however, does not permit not-for-profit agencies to give grants to for-profit businesses, although they are able to invest in such entities, which is what some had done in INDC. As a not-for-profit organization, TNI is legally entitled to receive grants from tax-free organizations and from government agencies. That meant that it could attract to the community resources that an ordinary for-profit business could not.

That organizational structure, of course, did have some disadvantages. For example, it was essential that the TNI budget be completely insulated from INDC's. That restriction reduces organizational flexibility, particularly in lean times. But if the funds were commingled, its not-for-profit status would be in jeopardy. Its tax status is an interesting wrinkle on organizational practice and worthy of attention. To describe it, however, is not to describe what the organization actually is and what it does.

Indeed, TNI is not easy to define. There is probably no organization quite like it anywhere. Its peculiar present shape is, in a sense, a consequence of its original and ambiguous mandate. The Neighborhood Institute was created to be a special kind of social service agency. To be sure, it was to provide some services associated with such agencies (for example, job counseling and training), but as an organization dreamed up out of the experience of the '60s, it was also expected to help organize the community around particular issues: that is, to be an unrepresentative representative of the relatively dispossessed.

There was some perception among TNI's leaders that the community needed greater mobilization of a sort that the traditional South Shore community organizations, with their focus on middle-class amenities, did not provide, and special leadership to look after the interests of those residents whose concerns were likely to be overlooked or maybe even harmed by the bank's activities.

Its first director was a visionary educator who had difficulty finding his footing in the unmarked terrain and soon moved on to an educational job in Florida. Grzywinski then brought in Fletcher, whom he had been wooing for five years, and, along with him, Michael Bennett, who had been a community organizer in Ohio before coming to Chicago as a student at the University of Chicago School of Social Service Administration, and who had worked with Grzywinski on the original INDC proposal. (Bennett later became TNI president when Fletcher left in 1983 to join the South Shore Bank.)

Although the original staff of TNI was composed of highly paid and talented professionals from the world of social services, as black people in a largely black South Shore they saw themselves as prima facie better representatives of the community than the people connected with the bank, and they took on some of the community's mood and style of mild alienation from the smooth and predominantly white world in which they saw the bank operating. Therefore, communication and cooperation among all the affiliates was probably not what it should have been. There was some reinventing of the wheel and a bit of unnecessary overlap. But it was a style that made TNI members sensitive to some of the community-based issues that might have been overlooked in the zeal to get a project moving.

As matters evolved, funding sources had much to do with the shift in the TNI mission. Supported heavily by the Charles Stuart Mott Foundation of Flint, Michigan, the staff initially planned efforts along a wide front. These included town meetings, the development of cultural programs, community organization around educational issues, an economic development program focusing on industrial development, job training and counseling, the protection of those displaced in the development process, harassment of slum landlords, and an array of housing services.

They themselves, however, felt harassed by the fact that they did not have a steady source of funds—most funding being on an annual basis—and a large proportion of their time was taken up making applications to foundations and government sources. The Mott Foundation, it should be pointed out, provided an important and stable funding base during those early years, and so to a lesser extent did the Chicago Community Trust.

In fact, TNI did attract substantial resources to South Shore. Between 1978 and 1980, the TNI budget rose from $167,700 to $943,400 before it turned downward to $847,600. Table 8.1 shows the level and sources of funding for that period.

This table shows that TNI was skillful at finding sources of funds and applying them to its broad general mandate. AMOCO funds, for example, went for a weatherization program, which became an early foundation for housing efforts. The EDA grant, though, was never able to produce the new industrial activity for which it was intended. Had TNI at that time worked more closely with the bank, the results might have been different.

Other grants made possible the beginnings of renovation for buildings turned over to TNI by HUD. Still others went for the diverse job training and placement services—in some cases as contracts with the relevant agencies.

The point is that, like the bank in its early days, TNI scrambled for resources while it tried to find a focus for its activities. Over time, the organization moved in what might be called a nuts-and-bolts direction as funding was not forthcoming for

Table 8.1

Sources and Amounts of Funding for TNI
(thousands of dollars)

	Year			
Source	1978	1979	1980	1981
Charles Stuart Mott Foundation	$178.8	$206.8	$178.5	$104.0
Chicago Community Trust		40.0	40.0	
AMOCO				150.0
U.S. Economic Development Authority			75.0	
U.S. Department of Human Services		88.7	324.1	206.2
U.S. Department of Housing				175.4
Illinois Board of Education		21.8	43.8	45.0
U.S. Department of Commerce			274.8	151.0

Source: INDC Annual Report, 1984.

more abstract and unmeasurable goals—cultural activities, the delivery of social services, and mobilization of the community. It was easier to perform jobs on a contractual basis with an agency or spend money on housing rehabilitation than to apply for grants for somewhat more nebulous social activities. Foundations often require new departures, dramatic short-term results, and they display a "show me" attitude toward recipients. Sometimes they simply get bored with supporting one organization year in and year out. No group can do long-term planning under those constraints.

Under the guidance of Robert Wordlaw, who joined TNI in 1978 from an employment training position in a city agency, the job training and placement program grew steadily with con-tracts from the city and the state—its major components being a GED program that relied on self-guided computer instruction and a clerical skills training program. In the 1979–1983 period, 740 people passed through that program, with 99 placed in jobs and another 74 continuing their education in some way. TNI has experimented as well with an apprenticeship program for those in the building trades. This effort grew out of the other node of growth in TNI's activities, housing.

TNI entered the housing world through what might be called the soft side. It took housing surveys; identified needs of resi-dents; helped harass landlords who were not maintaining buildings or were otherwise treating tenants poorly; provided assistance for South Shore residents looking for new, inexpen-sive housing; offered technical assistance to those trying to fix up their houses; provided a weatherization program for people trying to reduce heating costs; and, perhaps most impor-tant in those early days, worked closely with residents of the Parkside area, which was slated by the bank and City Lands for a huge development effort.

I will discuss the Parkside Partnership in more detail below. It is, however, essential to know at this point that City Lands, in partnership with RESCORP and the First National Bank of Chicago, planned a major $25 million redevelopment project, which included the purchase of twenty buildings with 446 units.

Although some of the buildings were, in fact, abandoned, and there was unprecedented expenditure for relocation by the Parkside Partnership itself, TNI took the responsibility of working with the people threatened with displacement, keeping them informed about what was happening and gaining their confidence; and working with local residents who owned the surrounding buildings—helping them to get rehabilitation loans and to participate in neighborhood activities that could maximize the positive spillover effects of the Parkside Partnership project.

The teamwork between the Parkside Partnership and TNI resulted in about one-third of those dislocated by the Parkside Project being rehoused in it. Others made smooth transitions to new locations. In addition, the owners of small three-flat and six-flat buildings were in a position to reap the advantages of this process rather than to have their property bulldozed.

It would be difficult to find anywhere a project of such magnitude that produced such a satisfactory outcome for so many people in a redevelopment target area. The Parkside effort brought to the fore Dorris Pickens, who early in 1986 succeeded Michael Bennett as TNI president. Pickens was trained as a schoolteacher and had been teaching in the Evanston schools when she and her husband moved to South Shore. She gave up teaching and found her way into the South Shore Bank. From there she moved into TNI. Although TNI had a trained housing specialist, she began to play an increasingly important role in housing matters. It was not long before TNI was involved in all aspects of the development of housing. Their involvement began in 1980, when the office took over a badly managed HUD building whose management they had been fighting with on behalf of the tenants.

As they committed themselves to entering housing in a big way, they were able to get control of an abandoned building which, with grants from the city and from HUD, they set out to rehabilitate as a sweat equity co-op. Financing included a Section 312 loan for $396,000, a block grant for $289,000, a development grant for $65,000, and $110,000 worth of labor or sweat equity. As Pickens said: "We began with the most idealistic, demanding and foolish goals: taking abandoned buildings and using them to provide home ownership for poor people."

That building was, in fact, renovated successfully, and other low-equity co-ops followed. Today, finding buildings in scavenger sales and other distressed areas and using funds from diverse sources—federal, city, and private—TNI is able to rehabilitate housing and bring it back into the mainstream. By 1985, TNI had five more buildings, with 126 units completed or in process.

Central to the process is Pickens, who is able to identify the diverse array of programs available to not-for-profit community-based organizations and to figure out how to assemble them.

What has happened to TNI, then, is that it has moved away from grants to fund its operations. Instead, its resources come from contracts from specific projects, either in the job training employment area or in the area of housing. Its officials still hold the ideal of helping the poorer components of the South Shore population. But with Michael Bennett's 1986 departure for the South Shore Bank as a commercial lending officer, TNI's program of community organizing has been left behind, as well as the broad thrust that included community education and culture within its mandate.

CITY LANDS

If TNI started out with a large and highly qualified staff and grand, complex goals that had to be tempered in the furnace of reality, the City Lands Corporation, a for-profit subsidiary of INDC, started quite modestly—with a staff of one and vague complex goals that also had to be tempered.

At its creation in 1978, City Lands was the object of a fantasy. If INDC could enter the real estate market early in its efforts, it would be able to "ride up" with the general property appreciation generated by INDC's efforts and therefore make profits for itself and for the community. Consequently, it was inadequately capitalized at $150,000, in the hope that it would quickly grow beyond that.

Alas, in the abstract almost everything sounds easier to do than it actually is in the concrete (no pun intended). In this case, it was even harder to do than it often is. To enter the real estate market in an economically marginal area is to enter a world of dramatically shifting and insecure terrain.

Ownership of property is often ambiguous because of tax sales and unpaid loans. Arson represents an attractive way to get out of a jam. Upwardly mobile first-time property owners sometimes display a crafty suspiciousness that makes negotiation difficult, and, at any rate, negotiation does not take place through established channels or follow established procedures. In rental property, economically marginal people whose capacity to generate monthly rent is variable often are delinquent and/or rent out rooms in their apartments in order to make ends meet. There are socially marginal people whose personal habits are not conducive to either the comfort or feelings of security of their neighbors or the long-range physical maintenance of facilities. This is not to suggest that most residents of low-income communities are alcoholics, criminals, or in other ways undesirable. But the proportion of such people is high enough so that landlords must be tough and careful about the maintenance of standards so that they can collect rent, especially when they have concerns about the economic future of their property and the community.

The first director of City Lands was Tom Gallagher. Gallagher had been a carpenter, a contractor, and work supervisor for one of the large condominium converters in the city. The choice of Gallagher represented a misperception of the skills needed to run the organization. Rather than somebody who knew buildings and how to build and repair them, City Lands needed an entrepreneur who could find investors, lenders, and developers and put together deals.

Under Gallagher's leadership in 1978 and 1979, City Lands supervised the rehabilitation of bank-owned property, in order to enlarge the bank and to place a renovated storefront in the bank's building. They took over one abandoned building and rehabilitated it for condominium use, and worked to gain control of and manage a number of other buildings. Like other condominium projects in South Shore that did not do well, the City Lands effort was not very successful. A market never materialized for the condo building. It stood there under-utilized and draining the corporation's limited resources. Other attempts to purchase buildings and fix them up for sale also did not work out very well. In some cases, City Lands had difficulty getting control of and closing deals on buildings, and in others seemed not to be able to move on the buildings it did own. The company was simply not familiar enough with the marketplace and did not have the contacts or capital to make quick deals at advantageous prices so that it could profit in a weak market.

South Shore was still, in those days, an area from which investors and lenders stayed away. Under Gallagher, City Lands never devised a mechanism to finance its deals in a section where conventional credit was not available, and South Shore Bank financing was denied to City Lands.

Gallagher did lay the groundwork, however, for what was to become City Lands' and INDC's most important undertaking: the Parkside Partnership project. The key partners in the deal were City Lands, RESCORP, and First Chicago Neighborhood Development Corporation, a subsidiary of Chicago's First National Bank. Targeted to deal with what had become the most massively deteriorated area of South Shore, Parkside, it ultimately transformed the entire area. Abandoned buildings were restored. All the other structures in the project were rehabilitated, their exteriors sandblasted and decorated with gleaming black iron gates and grilles, which had almost become a RESCORP symbol. With its views of Chicago's Jackson Park, a creative use of public space for malls, and banners hanging from the lampposts to announce a new neighborhood, Parkside no longer hinted that it was once South Shore's sorriest section. Like RESCORP's 1974–1978 projects, this one had positive spillover effects far beyond the effort itself. Construction began in 1980, and renovation began in earnest on many nearby buildings, so that by the end of 1985, dreadfully unmaintained structures were the exception rather than the rule.

The execution of that project, however, was left to Gallagher's successor, for, as an educator was found to be an inap-

propriate leader for what TNI was to become, a contractor and
work supervisor was not quite what City Lands needed. City
Lands began to take off only when it was taken over by somebody who could put together complex deals and also be a tough
building manager. Like Pickens and so many other top INDC
people, Sara Lindholm, who replaced Gallagher in 1979, came
to INDC from an unlikely direction. A graduate student in
Indian history at the University of Chicago, she first worked
for the South Shore Study project. From there she went to
work for the South Shore Bank in the real estate department
and left to join Gallagher at City Lands.

She set out to put City Lands on a firm financial basis. She
found the company overextended in many directions with no
clear plan for properties it had options on or, in fact, already
owned. The first step, then, was to scale back staff and programs, while instituting more sophisticated financial controls.
Her efforts included renting up or selling to investors the units
in the failed condominium; selling buildings for which there
was no economic plan; finding investors for a small 13-unit
Section 8 project; and assembling, for fee income, the buildings
for a large Section 8 project of another developer in the Bryn
Mawr West section of South Shore, just south of Parkside.

At the same time, she familiarized herself with the way
orthodox developers operated and became part of the development world, learning how to use subsidies skillfully and how
to find financing. One of her particularly important tools was
syndication of partnership interest in subsidized rehabilitation
projects.

By 1985, City Lands had completed four profitable years,
had seven buildings (190 units) under construction, and was
negotiating for financing on four others (195 units). Another
large housing project was in the pipeline. The recipient of a
$4,300,000 HODAG (Housing Development Action Grant), it
still faced South Shore's major financial problem, finding
appropriate private credit arrangements. It was not until June
1987 that the project finally closed.

Projects like these take years even to get started. To the
extent that they are subsidized, they often require layers of

bureaucratic approval from city, state, and federal government. In addition, the local political process must be honored. The local alderman has to be persuaded that the project is in the community's interest and does not have substantial and politically important opposition.

Many projects must also have community approval before there is an official sign-off on them. Late in 1985, City Lands was on the edge of closing a major deal on Seventy-first Street. It involved the construction of a 111,300-square-foot convenience shopping center or mini-mall, anchored by a 64,000-square-foot supermarket. Although the city had yet to purchase the property at that time, City Lands had been developing it for four years. The effort included trying to attract developers of other mini-malls throughout the city, making subsidy arrangements—in this case a UDAG for $1,200,000—finding financing, and getting city approval.

City Lands has the commitment of one of the region's large supermarket chains. If the project succeeds, it would be the first chain to enter the heart of South Shore after fifteen years of supermarket disinvestment in the area. Most of the land is already vacant commercial space—some is the site of an old army recruiting center—but it does include some housing units. There have been numerous hearings on the project as well as approvals and withdrawals of approval over a period of three years. Some groups of local residents opposed the project, and, as a consequence, there were several rounds of public hearings. From the City Lands perspective, it seemed as if it were being asked three times to demonstrate that there was broad public approval of the project.

The city government then decided not to move ahead with the purchase. Again, political resources were mobilized, and the city government reversed itself. The project still needs more approvals before site acquisition can begin. No ordinary for-profit developer would have persisted so long.

As is always the case when there are resources to be given out, both Pickens and Lindholm must deal with community activists who at times look as if they want a piece of the pie in order to remain silent. For example, one leader, whose own buildings have been in housing court for code violation, may complain on one day that South Shore is a solid middle-class community and that to bring in subsidized housing is to drag the community down, and on another that such big-time outside entrepreneurs as City Lands are picking off the good housing in a black community and creating problems for the poor residents.

Many of his appeals are to people outside the South Shore world, who have difficulty evaluating what is happening internally and are susceptible to racially based pleas. As is true with so much else that happens in South Shore, issues of this sort get fought out in forums located far from the community.

City Lands and TNI are having a dramatic impact on the South Shore housing scene. There are many levels of complexity in achieving housing development. In many instances, only a developer who does not have income goals as a primary consideration would continue to fight for projects in the face of credit difficulties, bureaucratic labyrinths, and the quirks of local politics. Those INDC affiliates provide the aggressive development behavior that it is impossible for a bank to carry out, and, because of their commitment to South Shore, they stick to their development agenda with levels of persistence uncommon in either business organizations or those in the not-for-profit sector.

SEVENTY-FIRST STREET

Despite what seem to be substantial gains in the physical setting of the community, the specter of Seventy-first Street continues to haunt the development process.

One student, recently asked to observe the street for a course, reported:

Generally, the area appears to be having some economic difficulties. There are numerous "for rent" signs and a large number of vacant store front businesses on the major shopping strip. . . . There was a large number of people, all black, walking around the neighborhood. Nevertheless, very few seemed to be shopping (they did not have packages and most businesses were empty). The economic difficulties of the small shop owners was symbolically represented by a sign in one of the stores stating "Closing Sale—Everything Must Go."

Interestingly, only a few stores seemed to be owned by blacks. Most shops were owned by individuals of Vietnamese or Korean descent. [This is not, strictly speaking, correct. It is an interesting perception.] However, they did not appear to be surviving any better than black shop owners. Their stores were empty and they appeared very anxious to sell me items.

. . . Litter was on the streets primarily in the form of paper. Paper from fast food restaurants or from candy. Sidewalks had cracks in them and seemed in need of repair. Overall . . . maintenance seemed fairly poor. . . . (Laseter).

For at least twenty years, Seventy-first Street has not been the class shopping strip it once was. Although the vacancy rate varies, it is always high. Men stand on street corners drinking out of bottles in brown paper bags. An observant stroller can see drug sales taking place among the street's habitués. And down the center of the street runs the old Illinois Central Railroad track, filled with litter.

Some stores do well. The Walgreens pharmacy is usually packed with customers, as is another drugstore and liquor store combination. Over the past thirteen years, numerous small businesses have come and gone—some of them with loans from the South Shore Bank.

City Lands has one employee who has been devoting most of his time to Seventy-first Street. If the convenience shopping center is completed, the street may get a new chance. Outside planners as well have come to look. James Rouse, the well-known developer who planned Harbor Place in Baltimore and Faneuil Hall in Boston, was beguiled more by the country club park that stands at one end of the street than he was by the street itself. A new planner proposes, as an anchor at one end of the street, a branch of a downtown department store, and a large public market as an attraction farther along.

Chicago's old commercial strips are clearly a problem for many of its communities, especially for largely black ones. A study (1982) by Patricia Wittberg of selected Chicago shopping strips shows that, even holding income and length of residence constant for the surrounding areas, shopping strips in largely black neighborhoods do more poorly than those in ethnically defined ones. Black people are long-term Americans with distinctively American tastes, and there is little reason then for them to stay confined to their own neighborhoods. As pointed out earlier, because of long histories of discrimination and a tradition of shipping inferior goods to the ghetto, those people who can afford to prefer to shop alongside what might be called mainstream Americans rather than in their own residential locations. So far, there is no predominantly black area of the city with a shopping strip that carries the kinds of distinctive merchandise that will attract people from a wide area. Even if the merchandise were there, it is not clear that large numbers of white potential customers will shop in a primarily black area. In some sense, it is such a strip that outside planners are trying to create.

In short, in the face of overwhelming odds, the workers of INDC have not yet given up on Seventy-first Street. In part, they are forced to struggle with it, because the strip serves as a symbol for the entire area. Passers-through who might be potential residents or investors are discouraged by prospects when they see what the street has to offer. Residents who worry about the future of their community take cues about how the area is doing from the strip as well. They know that they have a nice house or apartment, and that their neighbors are fine, upstanding folks. But the sight of a decayed shopping strip, combined with the memory of deterioration in other black neighborhoods, produces a sense of precariousness which is reflected in their commitment to staying in that housing market and, when making investment decisions, thinking about it as a place with a future.

There is another reason why the staff of INDC persists. Many experts told them they could not run a successful bank in such a neighborhood. They have managed to do so. Many experts told them that with their limited resources, they could not have an impact on the economic future of the neighborhood. Yet, they have managed to do so. Seventy-first Street is just a little harder—another example of an almost intractable reality that persistence and intelligence will overcome.

9

Development Tactics
and the Development Process

The INDC has been remarkably, perhaps uniquely, successful. Doing development in a declining minority area is no easy matter. There are so many ways in which the cards are stacked against the areas: a city government that has written them off; residents who flee because they are fearful, and other people who refuse to move there; landlords, building managers, and realtors who decide that the only way to make money is to undermaintain their properties and exploit the fact of racial change; a general pattern of disinvestment, which includes decisions not to support new retail establishments, not to provide credit, and either to withdraw insurance or impose unusually high rates that discourage investments; a population whose income distribution is skewed in a low direction; the departure of jobs to the suburbs and the Sunbelt; and underclass residents, some of whom commit crimes, destroy property, misbehave publicly, and scare people away. To combat those "natural" social forces is a full-time job, and one that requires attacks on many fronts. The forces of deterioration never sleep, and those who wish to reverse that process, consequently, must be ceaselessly vigilant.

It would be difficult to find comparable success anywhere. It has been a slow process and an expensive one. Profitability took ten years to achieve at the South Shore Bank. Although there were modest fruits from their efforts after the first four or five years, it took six more before it became unambiguously clear that development was really happening. The development fight is not over yet. There are sections of South Shore that are further deteriorated today than when INDC purchased the bank. The area still has to contend with the El Rukns, a grown-up version of the Blackstone Rangers; outside investors who insist on treating their own properties as inner-city slums and hasten the process that they ostensibly fear; and commercial areas that are symbols of blight and decay. Even positive economic developments seem to have a negative side. For example, the successful Walgreens store, with its brick walls and steel gates, communicates to all future investors that its corner is a dangerous place. Nonetheless, the South Shore effort is a success, and is so on unusual terms.

First, the impulse for South Shore development comes from a private-sector operation without the resources or the power of government or even the almost limitless purses of some foundations.

Second, development has taken place without racial integration and the displacement that often follows from the integration effort. The South Shore population is more than 90 percent black, and INDC has never made integration an agenda item. This point is worth underscoring. Most people who think of successful development think of a market in which blacks and whites compete for property. This view is so prevalent that many who want to know "how South Shore is doing" will immediately ask about its racial balance.

Third, INDC itself is racially integrated. I have taken some pains to identify white and black members of the team, because I think that the level of integration is unusual and important. In addition, through the whole process there have often been white community members who have played roles both as community leaders and as troops in community organizations, even when they represented a small minority. No part of American society is color-blind. The capacity of whites and blacks to work easily together and on an equal footing is impressive and unusual.

Fourth, management is not doctrinaire. It is able to make use of private- and public-sector resources and is not committed to any one program. This flexibility means that solutions can be designed for particular problems rather than problems found to suit ready-made solutions and larger schemes. Pragmatic is an overused word, yet it is difficult to imagine a more appropriate one for the INDC effort.

It is important to understand that its pragmatism is undergirded by a measure of idealism and social commitment on an individual level as well. The INDC personnel work long hours and bounce back from failures because they have a sense of doing something socially worthwhile. Although they are reasonably well paid for their jobs, many are sought out by other organizations offering better paying and, in some instances, less personally demanding jobs, yet turnover is low. The INDC is able to attract good people because there are large numbers of such people out there who are not willing to sacrifice social idealism for a big pay check, nor do they wish to sacrifice a comfortable standard of living in the name of do-gooding. INDC is able to attract good people because, although it does not pay top dollar, it pays well while offering an individual a chance to work for the good of the larger society.

All too often, those who do community work are expected to do so at near poverty-level wages and are thought to be ineffective and soft. In the business world, idealism is coupled with woolly-headedness, or a lack of toughness. To watch Mary Houghton look at a business plan, Jim Fletcher evaluate a proposal to buy a company, Jim Bringley consider a mortgage request, Sara Lindholm deal with a tenant who does not pay the rent, or Bob Wordlaw talk to one of his job trainees who comes in unkempt is to know that these people display none of those attributes. They succeed because they apply tough business standards. Yet, their commitment to development is so strong that when they fail, they do not walk away. They try something else.

Is INDC replicable? What are the elements of its success, and can they be used elsewhere? Ideally, the way to answer these questions would be to find large numbers of similar groups, to compare them with each other, and see which elements seem essential to success and which elements are just accidental to INDC. Since there are no organizations with which to compare it, the crucial elements must be guessed at. INDC works for a number of reasons. Let me summarize what appear to be a few of the essential ones.

First, this is not a hit-and-run operation. The key actors have been involved in the process for thirteen years, gaining experience and abilities. In addition, there has been enough time for new people to emerge with highly honed skills: people like Pickens of TNI, Bringley of real estate lending, and Lindholm of City Lands, who learned the business from the ground up. There have also been realistically long time lines for these people first to try things, and, if they failed, to try something else; and second, to pursue projects that do not reach fruition until four or five years after their initiation.

It also means that solutions are tempered to the environment. Good ideas often do not work, yet they are no less good because they failed. By learning from failure, INDC has become more sophisticated about its environment.

What makes the extended time frame possible is the most important single fact about INDC: it has its own capital base and is, consequently, self-sustaining. It is an ongoing operation that does not have to go to the grant-giving world or to the federal government on an annual basis to justify its existence. It has time to do the hard, slow things and to devote all of its efforts to them without the distraction of annual proposals to prepare and without well-meaning amateurs looking over its shoulder and telling it how to do things.

Foundations require short-term performance or, at least, the illusion of it. Foundation moods change—what is hot one year may not be very interesting the next. Having a consistent capital base, INDC knows that it can do things that are not necessarily flashy, but that might lay the foundation for something else. All participants know that the effort is a continuing one, and that resources are not here today and gone tomorrow, and that they do not need to be used before an arbitrarily set deadline, as in government situations, or before asking for more.

Being self-sustaining does not mean that INDC officials can behave irresponsibly or are responsible to nobody. The INDC and each of its affiliates have boards of directors who oversee activities with varying degrees of diligence and independence. Often individuals of some standing, the directors have a sense of responsibility for what they supervise. In addition, some of them are investors and have distinctive corporate responsibility for the invested funds. Even without board supervision, there are constraints. As bankers and business people, they must maintain their capital base and keep it growing. If they fail to do so, they may face the possibility of economic failure and the personal liability that goes with it. They are not, by contrast, civil servants who can keep their jobs no matter what the outcome. They cannot be nine-to-fivers either. Few great things happen within the limits of the forty-hour week.

The same assurance of continued presence and resources is important to those outside the organization as well. Borrowers know that if they provide a sustained-quality performance, they can come back for more assistance. If they try to gain funds without producing, there is an organization ready to wring from them the funds owed.

The expectation of continuity is also important for outside investors. They know that they are dealing with an organization that is in for the long run, and that fact means that it is an organization one can deal with reasonably.

There is some argument within INDC about how important it is that capital base be lodged in a bank instead of, say, a credit union, or a venture-capital organization. My own view is that the bank is crucial for this type of operation for at least two reasons. The first is that everybody knows what a bank is and that it has a certain high symbolic standing. Nobody has to explain it to the neighborhood residents. Think of the resonance of the word *banker* and compare it to occupation labels like *venture capitalist, developer,* or even *credit union manager.* The outside world, the one with the big resources, understands what a bank is, too. Asked to deal directly with neighborhoods, most potential bearers of significant resources will back off. But a banker: that is a different story. They understand him or her and he or she understands them. The bank, then, becomes a broker between the community and the corporate world.

The second reason that some of the South Shore Bank people mention is that a retail bank keeps them in continuous touch with the community. They learn who the reliable actors are and how to support them in their efforts. They also learn which matters people care about and which do not make much difference.

Another element in understanding the success of INDC in the South Shore community is that the scale of the endeavor is appropriate to the problem. The South Shore Bank is situated in a community where it *is* possible to know the actors and to trace out the consequences of one's actions. Coins are not being cast into a vast and unknown sea.

Likewise, the amount of the resources available is not enough to allow developers to ride roughshod over people. The process is one of continuous negotiation with the environment. Local energies and participation are encouraged. The development process in South Shore, as I have shown, has not been fast. Its pace allows internal adjustments to be made by the residents as they adapt to the new reality and discover that they can have some impact on outcomes. They have time to make plans.

These considerations raise the issue of how a development organization relates to its community. I have pointed out that South Shore Bank has kept community organizations at arm's length and, by so doing, has gained a heightened capacity to act. The development of community organizations is alleged to be important for several reasons. The groups express the views of community residents, they prevent arbitrary and high-handed action, and they mobilize the community for political action. If a bank is working with the community on a daily basis, it has some idea about what residents think. Beyond that, it is not the bank's responsibility to generate political mobilization. There is real confusion here between that and economic mobilization. Because the bank is a bank and a skillfully run one, it has helped generate new investors in the community, many of whom are old community residents. Provided with adequate credit and some guidance, these small, locally grown operations become self-sustaining, producing new wealth and better housing for South Shore residents. This is economic, as compared to political, mobilization.

The third element is that INDC's biggest achievement is the mobilization of fresh resources brought to the community from the outside after a period in which those who controlled resources placed their funds elsewhere.

I discussed in chapter 1 the analogy to third-world economic development, the temptation to think of local urban communities as relatively closed systems. But neighborhoods are not self-sufficient kingdoms. People earn and spend their money outside them. Much of what happens to them depends on decisions made elsewhere. To make policy on the understanding of those neighborhoods as small, self-sufficient units is to decree to them a standard of living appropriate to the seventeenth century.

As far back as Adam Smith, individuals understood that the division of labor was responsible for increasing society's wealth, and that the division of labor can succeed only in augmented market areas. Consequently, a ruler who wants his region to grow economically should create conditions of easy transportation and communication within it. In like manner, someone concerned with urban economic development is interested in facilitating the flow of resources and people into and out of the neighborhood. This not only increases efficiency but brings essential resources into the neighborhood. The neighborhood that is a target for development is historically a place that resources have passed by—that is what disinvestment is all about.

To tell a poor community to ignore the outside world and tend its own gardens, or even to start its own solar energy programs (less attractive when oil is $10 a barrel, as compared to $40), or even to rehabilitate each other's houses is almost pointless.

The trick, then, is to reverse that process and bring resources back into the community.

This is where the INDC is preeminent. In conjunction with community residents, it brought into the community the funds of the investors who purchased the bank, the money of

development depositors, the resources of developers such as
RESCORP and First Chicago Neighborhood Development Corporation, other new lenders and investors involved in City
Lands projects, and the resources of federal and state agencies.
These resources were used both for such infrastructural improvements as streets and sidewalks and such parks as the
South Shore County Club Park, and as straight subsidies for
housing construction and employment training. It is not easy
to add all that up. But the figure can be no less than
$150,000,000.

INDC succeeded in attracting millions of dollars because
all of its early leaders had extensive city, state, and national
contacts from previous activities. For example, Grzywinski's
ties to IHDA helped bring RESCORP into the community.
Milton Davis was able to use his connections with city government to bring trees to Seventy-first Street. Heagy, who had
worked for First National, was instrumental in encouraging
that bank's investment in the Parkside Partnership. Where
those ties did not exist, they were self-consciously cultivated.
Lindholm, for example, built relations with downtown developers and suppliers of financial resources. Warren (1975)
has suggested that minority communities are often hampered
in dealing with their problems by a lack of connection to the
larger world. Because of INDC's leadership, South Shore did
not have that problem.

The funds brought into the community were not just thrown
into a South Shore rathole. The fact that South Shore is not
an isolated and self-sufficient community cuts both ways. All
the projects resulted in increased citywide employment; they
resulted in increased demand for raw materials, none of which
are purchased in South Shore; in a whole new range of investment opportunities provided for those outside the community
looking for a decent rate of return on their dollars; and in
properties taxable at higher rates to pay for city services. This
last point is important. In my studies of other similar Chicago
communities, the story of tax delinquency is cumulative and
depressing. The number of delinquencies grow, and those properties that become delinquent do not get redeemed. In South

Shore the number of delinquencies has declined substantially since 1973, and of those the number of buildings that do pay their taxes before three years have passed has increased. This is possible only when market forces are moving in a positive direction. Cities or parts of cities get attention only when they generate new wealth (Molotch, 1978). The INDC has brought that attention back to South Shore.

Indeed, INDC's biggest achievement is not a simple and direct consequence of its own investment activity. Because it is a corporation with an active and complex agenda in the community, it has made the possibility of investment seem real to outsiders. Its activity generated all the other—that is, in the language of the smart-money folks, the INDC investment created impressive leverage.

This is a more complicated point than it might seem. People cannot simply open a dummy bank in a neighborhood and invite the world in to invest. One must invest in the neighborhood oneself and have a string of successes that make other investment possibilities credible. And one must have the knowledge of the community that comes from working in it to pass on to potential investors.

As we have seen, the South Shore Bank has lent $51,600,000 (much of which comes from outside the community) for the purchase and rehabilitation of property alone. That kind of activity by itself would not have led to the measurable upgrading of South Shore. In the face of decline, a neighborhood like South Shore needs a resource jolt of substantial magnitude in order to reverse the powerful downward-pulling forces. It is only by actively conducting affairs in a way that both shows commitment and makes sense to the business world and by demonstrating that its managers have the capacity to perform, that INDC is itself in the position to make a marriage: that is, to become a broker between the community and a range of other investors.

The INDC officials know their community and know how to mobilize resources within it. They know the successful investors, and they know what is politically viable. They have increasingly learned how to navigate in a world that had been terra incognita to similar institutions. Consequently, they became a link from one world to the other. In some instances, they do that directly by moving resources. In other cases, they provide explanations that make it possible for others to join that world themselves. Furthermore, they call attention to a world that others may not even have had on their maps.

There are other components that go into INDC success. As discussed in chapter 2, there was its decision to undertake its efforts in a community that was not massively deteriorated. South Shore provided an underlying resource base to build on. In addition, the South Shore community is situated near another, Hyde Park, that is in strong economic condition. How much that contributes to its success may yet be seen. In 1985, INDC extended its operations to the Austin community in Chicago, which is in far further deteriorated condition with much higher rates of tax delinquency, unemployment, and building abandonment. It starts with far more resources in hand than when it began in South Shore. More importantly, it brings thirteen years of experience to the development effort. Whether it can overcome the powerful forces of neglect in Austin remains to be seen.

Another component is the multipronged organizational structure INDC developed. It is not clear that that is the particular structure needed in all development settings. The South Shore model emphasizes real estate development, an appropriate approach for a bedroom community. Other systems may be more appropriate to job creation. What does seem clear is that a bank by itself cannot do comprehensive development. It relies on people walking in the door to ask for loans, and that is a severe limitation. Other agencies that approach development far more aggressively are essential, and INDC has created them.

Finally, I repeat, most INDC personnel are not orthodox bankers. They are smart people found in other worlds, trained by management, and then encouraged to be creative. There is the sense that because they come to the task with few preconceptions, they are able to forge new instruments and devise new tactics. That orientation toward recruitment may not be essential for success, but it is an ingredient of the South Shore effort.

In short, by beginning with a solid capital base lodged in an institution—in this case a bank—that the business and public worlds understand, INDC is able to go about its work in a tough-minded and professional way. This is an opportunity available to few development organizations. What this one has shown is that areas neglected by traditional sources of revenue can, in fact, be revitalized. The process is a long and slow one and involves bringing those sources of revenue back to the community. It can be done only with resources that allow mistakes and experimentation over a protracted period of time, and with an organizational structure that permits a multidimensional solution to a problem that has multiple causes.

Glossary

CD: certificate of deposit

CDH: Chicago Department of Housing

Chicago Community Trust: a Chicago-based foundation

Chicago United: an association of community-affairs and race-relations officials from some of Chicago's major corporations

CHS: Chicago Department of Human Services

CNA: a large national insurance corporation

EDA: Economic Development Authority

FHA: Federal Housing Administration

HODAG: Housing Development Action Grant

IHDA: Illinois Housing Development Authority

Local Area Development Corporation: a citizens' group that has the legal capacity to lend out SBA funds at a subsidized rate

MGIC: Milwaukee Guarantee Insurance Company, a mortgage insurance company

National Tea: a large chain of supermarkets that closed all of its Chicago stores in 1977

O'Keeffe: a subneighborhood of South Shore

Parkside: a subneighborhood of South Shore, consisting primarily of rental units

Parkside Partnership: joint undertaking of City Lands, RESCORP, and the First Chicago Neighborhood Development Corporation to rehabilitate what had been South Shore's most badly deteriorated section

Phoenix Partnership: a group of investors organized by Steve Perkins in 1976 in an attempt to focus development activities on Seventy-first Street

RESCORP: a consortium of over fifty savings and loan associations aiming to invest in urban redevelopment projects

SBA: Small Business Administration

TACH: Technical Assistance Corporation for Housing

References

Anderson, Elijah. 1978. *A Place on the Corner*. Chicago: University of Chicago Press.

Caplowitz, David. 1967. *The Poor Pay More: Consumer Practices of Low-Income Families*. New York: Free Press.

Cole, John A., Alfred L. Edwards, Earl G. Hamilton, and Lucy J. Reuben. Summer 1985. "Black Banks: A Survey and Analysis of the Literature." *Review of Political Economy*. 14(1): 29–50.

Hannerz, Ulf. 1969. *Soul Side: Inquiries into Ghetto Culture and Community*. New York: Columbia University Press.

Hoyt, Homer. 1942. "South Shore." In *Forty-four Cities in the City of Chicago*. Chicago: Chicago Planning Commission.

Kuhn, Thomas. 1962. *Structure of Scientific Revolution*. Chicago: University of Chicago Press.

Laseter, Robert. Spring 1986. Fieldwork assignment, University of Chicago.

Liebow, Elliot. 1967. *Tally's Corner*. Boston: Little, Brown.

Molotch, Harvey. 1972. *Managed Integration: Doing Good in the City*. Berkeley: University of California Press.

———. 1976. "The City as Growth Machine: Toward a Political Economy of Place." *American Journal of Sociology* 82(2): 309–32.

Otti, Phyllis Betts. 1978. "The Nature and Dynamics of Local Black Activism in an Urban Area: The Case of South Shore." Ph.D. dissertation, University of Chicago.

Taub, Richard P., and Doris L. Taub. 1974. *American Society in Tocqueville's Time and Today*. Chicago: Rand-Mc-Nally.

Taub, Richard P., D. Garth Taylor, and Jan D. Dunham. 1984. *Paths of Neighborhood Change*. Chicago: University of Chicago Press.

Warren, Donald. 1975. *Black Neighborhoods: An Assessment of Community Power*. Ann Arbor: University of Michigan Press.

Whyte, William F. 1955. *Street Corner Society*, 2d ed. Chicago: University of Chicago Press.

Wittberg, Patricia. Summer 1982. "Neighborhood Shopping Areas in Eight Chicago Neighborhoods: An Exploration of Variations." Ph.D. dissertation, University of Chicago.

Woodstock Institute. 1982. *Evaluation of the Illinois Neighborhood Development Corporation*.

Index